# PASTORAL CARE IN THE
# MODERN HOSPITAL

# PASTORAL CARE
## IN THE
# MODERN HOSPITAL

HEIJE FABER

SCM PRESS LTD

Translated by Hugo de Waal from the Dutch
*de pastor in het moderne ziekenhuis*
Van Gorcum & Co. n.v., Assen 1968

334 01207 4

*First published in English 1971*
*by SCM Press Ltd*
*56 Bloomsbury Street London*

© *SCM Press Ltd 1971*

*Printed in Great Britain by*
*Western Printing Services Limited*
*Bristol*

# CONTENTS

# CONTENTS

# PREFACE

When one begins to write a book about pastoral care in the modern hospital, it comes as a surprise to discover that there is virtually no literature in the field. One is setting out on a journey through uncharted country and without guides. Apart from some fairly general articles and some printed lectures, together with a few vague directions in books on pastoralia, I have not succeeded in finding any publications on the subject.

This confirms some observations made by Elizabeth Barnes in her book *People in Hospital*, which was written on the basis of the findings of a large number of international study groups. She quotes from one report:

The role of the religious counsellor or spiritual guide in general hospital therapy is understood by only a few people . . . embarrassment and reluctance among hospital staff . . . the failure of the religious institutions and their official representatives to communicate what it is they have to say and hope to do.[1]

There is no clear picture of the role of the minister in the hospital, and remarkably little study has been devoted to it. On the whole, it would seem that the minister is felt to be – in the words of one hospital director – an 'alien body' by the hospital staff.

We might perhaps say that while the minister is formally accepted in the hospital, he is nevertheless not 'noticed', and hence has no clearly defined place – often, in fact, he has no room or staff. This is partially, at any rate, because his work is little understood. For the minister himself this raises some significant problems. He comes to realize that his place in the hospital rests on weak foundations: in the progressive secularization of society, which affects the hospital deeply, how long can he count on the place he has at present? He asks himself whether this place is perhaps his at present only because of a kind of 'guilt feeling' on the part of the medical staff, which is aware of its one-sided relationship with the patients. But how long will this last? He realizes that he must clarify his place and role in the hospital both to himself and to the hospital staff, not only in order to keep his position, but in order to fulfil his task properly. In so doing he will also need to integrate his place and role into the whole complex of the staff through good contacts. Finally, to clarify is not all. He will also have to make his role credible. His behaviour at the sick-bed and his attitude towards the medical and nursing staff are matters of even greater importance.

The present book is in effect a revision of an earlier publication of mine, *Problemen rond het Ziekbed* (Problems of the sick-bed), published in 1959, which was read outside clergy circles and was, for example, used in training courses for nurses. It sold out, and when the publishers asked me to consider a new edition, I came to the conclusion that the time was ripe for a revision. The first edition mirrored the situation of the time. A great deal has happened since then. On the one hand the problems of the modern hospital have become much clearer; at the same time, we are seeing a thorough reappraisal of the identity of the clergyman in modern society influenced considerably by the 'clinical training' approach which is now also spreading to the Netherlands. It seemed to me that this book would be more to the point if I paid more attention to these two aspects. Hence it has been written with not only the minister but also the doctor and nurse in mind; it may perhaps even be of service to the sick. In this way, an entirely new work has emerged, incorporating only a few brief extracts from the first edition. I have, however, made use of various articles and lectures on the subject which I have given in the last few years. I would like to thank Dr M. W.

Jongsma, Director of the Akademische Ziekenhaus in Leiden,
both for reading through part of the manuscript and for many
helpful comments. Finally, a great deal is said in this book about
the female nurse. I realize that there are also male nurses.

# I

# The Problem of the Sufferer

The title of this chapter might well make one ask whether it is right to think of one who suffers as a 'problem'. Surely he has the right to call on our care and help, and surely, to make him into a problem is a sign of insensitivity to the call which he makes and has every right to make?

It is nevertheless a fact of history that this has by no means been man's natural reaction to the sufferer everywhere and at all times. It can be argued from history that the sufferer causes a kind of fear among his fellow-men, which has made them remove him from their company rather than care for him. Those familiar with the Eastern world will know how even today there is an indifference towards sufferers; it is not unknown simply to let them die by the roadside. It would appear that care for the suffering is linked with certain basic attitudes which are part of our culture, but are either not present in other cultures or find a different expression.

It is therefore arguable that the sufferer presents his fellow-men with a problem because he arouses ambivalent feelings. In this book I am concerned to show that this ambivalence is still present in our twentieth-century society, and that doctors, ministers and nurses sense this in the background of their work.

The attitude of a society towards its sick is thus linked to its cultural pattern, that complex of ideas, customs and emotions by which it is ruled and by which those brought up within it are inescapably influenced. It will be useful at this point to glance at the attitude towards the sick of a so-called 'primitive' society. The sick man will be regarded as under the spell of evil powers. His recovery – i.e. his restoration to the normal community of the tribe – will be a question of magic. He is therefore a source of danger, not to be lightly approached; people are afraid of him. Often this entails his exclusion from the community; he is moved to the 'outside', to a house apart. This reaction to the sick man who belongs 'outside', and the emotional desire to reject him, are still in evidence in Western society. In the village communities of my childhood the mentally sick – in fact anyone behaving abnormally – would be ridiculed; it is worth noticing our own use of words such as 'lunatic'.

Florence Nightingale spent her life seeking to overcome an attitude which banished the sick from society and scarcely bothered even to treat them. Books such as C. S. Forester's *Hornblower* series, which give vivid descriptions of the seaman's lot in the time of Napoleon, show only too clearly the primitive approach to the care of the sick at that time. Even if the churches took this care upon themselves and equipped institutions of their own, it was nonetheless on the assumption that the sick were like beggars, the outcasts of society, to whom Christ's church was called to minister.

If we turn from there to the modern hospital, we shall clearly recognize that in our culture far-reaching changes have taken place in society's attitude to the sick. Instead of putting away the sick, keeping them out of sight, the modern emphasis is on treatment: where many patients previously could not even be treated because of simple lack of medical knowledge, now the whole system is geared to cures. The expansion of medical and technical knowledge has fundamentally altered our approach to the sick. It has created the possibility of treating the sick man as a 'normal' person and not as an outsider, as one who does belong, even though for a time he is out of action. This recognition of our common humanity with the sick, of the man, the person in him, is of course what Christian compassion has always taught. It is what the humanizing forces in our society have striven for.

It has been made possible through the development of our culture. We are justified in stressing the importance of cultural attitudes both in the change of attitude towards the sick and in the consequent development of the hospital. If we are to understand the factors at work here, and hence to gain some insight into the way things are likely to develop and into the problems which are likely to arise, we shall do well to study more deeply the influence of cultural patterns.

Our glance at a primitive society will give us a useful perspective on our own situation. In primitive cultures we are dealing with closed societies; the physical and spiritual boundaries within which the tribe lives are clearly defined. Within those boundaries community life is highly structured; every aspect of life is governed by rules – explicit or implicit – and these are often both imposed and supported by a strong hierarchical structure. Undergirding the whole structure is the conviction that this whole order of things is essentially religious; to take part in the life of the community is to share in a divine order. Clearly, the individual who does not conform is not only marked as an outsider but also presents a threat to the divine order. He does not belong to it; therefore he belongs to the demonic world. In such a society it is clear that the sick will be experienced as outsiders, not conforming, dangerous and threatening. They are those who have fallen out of the divine order; they stand under the influence of demons.

This attitude towards the sick survived into modern times. The sick stand under the influence of evil spirits (a concept to be found in both the Old and New Testaments): these spirits have to be banished (exorcism); charms can protect one against sickness. It is, however, important to recognize that such an attitude towards the sick is closely linked with the place the sick have in society. They do not belong; they are the outcasts. We may well find examples of this in our own neighbourhood: outside the walls of some of our biggest cities and towns there will be isolation hospitals, to which those suffering from contagious diseases were once banished. The leper had to announce his presence in the street by waving a rattle. In the New Testament, again, we find a number of examples of this attitude towards lepers. In Isa. 53.2f. we can see how in ancient Israel the healthy regarded one who was sick:

He had no form or comeliness that we should look at him, and no beauty that we should desire him. He was despised and rejected by men; a man of sorrows, and acquainted with sickness; and as one from whom men hide their faces he was despised and we esteemed him not.

Again, when Job is covered in sores, he sits among the ashes and is virtually rejected by his wife.

There is a good example of the way in which primitive cultures treat the sick, and how healing is brought to them, in an essay by Clifford Geertz in the collection *Anthropological Approaches to the Study of Religion*. Geertz describes the healing rites practised by the Navaho tribe. After two stages, of purification and of prayer for the recovery of the sick man, the curing ritual moves into a rite of identification of the sick man with the Holy People. The sick man is laid on a sand-painting depicting the people, and pressed down until the pattern of his body is imprinted on this picture: thus he is accepted into the society of his people and there takes place 'a bodily identification of the human with the divine'.[1] Clearly, in this whole attitude towards the sick there is a fear of that which the sick man represents. It is the fear of the other and of the danger that the other threatens. The smaller the society and the more closed the circle, the greater the fear of the other: a psychologist will bear witness to this. Every closed society will hide within itself a certain amount of repressed fear and aggression. This fear and aggression are projected in its attitude towards the sick. Hence all the defence mechanisms that come into play towards the sick: the sick have to be isolated and, if possible, made to look ridiculous.

If the attitude towards the sick in the cultural milieu of a small primitive society can be understood in these terms, we should be able to see that traces of a similar attitude are present later – maybe even in our own time. We have already pointed out the urge to ridicule the mentally abnormal. We may perhaps find that even in our own time there is a need to isolate the sick; this may well mask a deeper need to defend ourselves against him. Later in this book we will examine this possibility more closely. However, even if we do recognize traces of this primitive defensive attitude today, it is nevertheless clear that in our own society we are dealing with a different cultural pattern and, in consequence, with a different approach towards the sick. There has undoubtedly been a change of attitude in the West towards suffering and towards those who suffer. We can describe this change as a form of 'demythologizing'. The sick are no longer regarded as 'demonic'. Two figures are of decisive importance in this development: Hippocrates and Christ. Hippocrates is regarded as the founder of modern medicine. In his view, disease is the result of natural causes, and in fact he laid the foundation of scientific research into the causes of sickness. He lived between 460 and 377 BC and by his approach broke through the primitive magic concepts of healing. Some quotations from Hippocrates make his position clear:

It seems to me that this sickness (epilepsy) is just as divine as all the others: they are all equally divine in origin, because all have a natural origin, without which no illness comes into being.

And again:

On the contrary, I believe that it is not possible to gain a reliable knowledge of human nature in any other way than through the art of healing. It is only when we have mastered the whole of this art in all its aspects, that we can come to such knowledge . . . It seems essential to me, that every physician has a good knowledge of (human) nature; if he wishes to fulfil his task properly, he must zealously strive to understand how man reacts to eating and drinking and other events in his life and, moreover, to understand how these things influence one another. He who does not know what the effect on man is of every thing, will neither learn to understand the consequences, nor be able to give a proper prescription.

And finally:

For everything that happens one can find a cause. Clearly chance has no place, except as a name, in the presence of causality. The art of healing clearly consists in a search for causes, and this will always be so.

This vision also governed his treatment of the sick; with him the modern approach to medical research and therapy begins. For Hippocrates, the one who suffers is, in principle, no longer under the influence of demons and therefore rejected from society. He has rather become a neutral object, to be treated by a doctor. We should understand, however, that this was a change in principle only. For even after Hippocrates there is still a sense of the 'alien' about suffering and the sufferer. Even if this attitude has been modified, we still find a projection of man's own fears and uncertainties in his attitude towards the sick.

The impact of Christ is more indirect. It is that his whole approach to life, including its suffering, has removed the demonic aspect of suffering. He is the one who takes suffering upon himself and thereby makes it possible to approach suffering in a different way. The early Christians saw in the sufferings of Christ a fulfilment of Isa. 53. Here it is said of the man of sorrows, the sufferer, that

He has borne our sicknesses and carried our sorrows . . . that he was oppressed and afflicted . . . they made his grave with the wicked . . . but the will of the Lord will prosper in his hands.

On this view, his suffering gains a positive meaning for the community and has a place in the purpose of God. It becomes possible to claim fellowship with this 'outcast', as indeed later martyrs did. It is clear that in this way suffering is removed from the sphere of the demonic. Thus those who were sick became in principle approachable as 'members of the community': they could become the object of Christian compassion, and hence people to be cared for and nursed.

It is important to recognize that the modern hospital has its origin in this attitude towards the sick. It was originally not 'an institution for diagnosis, treatment and nursing', which would be the modern definition of a hospital, but rather a place in which works of mercy and compassion could be performed. Those works were: to feed the hungry, to give the thirsty drink, to clothe the naked, to bury the dead, to give shelter to the traveller, to comfort the sick, to set free the imprisoned, and to bring compassion even to the incurably sick, whom Hippocrates left to his lot. Thus the sick are still 'different'; sometimes they are still regarded as 'sinful' (under the influence of evil spirits) – witness the belief in the power of witches to make people sick – but the first big step towards the 'demythologizing' of our attitude towards the sick has been taken.

We see, then, in Hippocrates and Christ two important influences in the shaping of our modern culture and in our change in attitude towards suffering and those who suffer. They have brought about a gradual rejection of the demonic theory, and with it have brought about an increase in concentration on proper care, diagnosis and therapy. It was to be centuries before this change really became dominant, and we must recognize that even today there are traces of a more primitive attitude. The feeling that the sick are in some way 'foreign' is one we still find at certain points in our approach to them. Fortunately, the nastier expressions of this, such as our treatment of the mentally ill, who could still in 1850 be described as guilty of contact with evil spirits, have wholly disappeared.

This development in our cultural attitude has left its mark on the hospitals. We may perhaps say that the changes in the nature of hospitals over the ages afford us a fairly accurate index of the changes in our society's attitude to the suffering.

Admission to hospital is no longer a question of compassion for the poor, but has become a purely medical concern. Thus the modern hospital has finally broken with its origins as a refuge for the poor who could find nowhere else to lay his head, when sickness afflicted him.[2]

As treatment in sickness is no longer seen as a favour, but as a right guaranteed by the law of the land, the view of it as care for the poor disappears. Henceforth development of the hospital runs parallel with the development of medical science, and is often outstripped by it.

# 2

# The Problem of the Hospital

Anyone taking a closer look at the modern hospital will quickly realize that a discussion of radical importance has developed over the past few years about the nature of hospital life. This has an important bearing on pastoral ministry in the hospital.

The modern hospital is a highly complicated affair in which personal commitment to and close contact with a great variety of one's fellow-men, hovering between hope and fear, is regulated by and caught in the highly specialized machinery of the whole process of treatment and nursing. Here we have a close-meshed network of spaces, apparatus, specialized tasks, hierarchical relationships, horizontal and vertical lines of communication, shared responsibilities, unassailable expertise, prized status relationships and prestige structures full of latent conflict. Here we have a restless atmosphere in which sharply timed procedures and techniques demanding scrupulous care place all those taking part at times in an almost tangible nervous tension with one another . . . If the priest in this modern hospital is going to make a fruitful contribution and is going to find himself secure in his role, he will have to have more than a superficial understanding of his own position in this social structure and he will have to be highly sensitive to the socio-psychological conditions in which he is to operate.[1]

Where, then, in his 'role' does the minister meet the problem posed by the modern hospital? In a little book which is full of wit and at the same time very much to the point, *What's Wrong with Hospitals?*, the English journalist, Gerda L. Cohen, has described her experiences as a patient in hospital, experiences which she later followed up, explored and tested through many discussions and conversations in various hospitals.[2]

It is already clear from her Preface what it is that particularly irritates her. Patients don't count. They are often needlessly humiliated and as a result they become more and more frustrated. What strikes her forcibly is the lack of contact between the patient on the one hand and the various members of the hospital staff on the other. She attributes this to three causes: first, the past history of hospitals, in which the patient was the poor man who had to be grateful that anyone was prepared to care for him at all; secondly, the hospital hierarchy which operates like a sort of caste-system in which the patient belongs somewhere at the bottom of the ladder; thirdly, the development of medical treatment with its increasingly clear accent on specialization and the consequent dehumanization of the patient. In other words, in hospital the patient is above all treated as an object to be diagnosed, to be treated, to be nursed, to be fed and to be kept clean, etc. We must add to that the fact that the patient has been removed from the society to which he is accustomed and has been in a sense isolated; visitors represent an unwelcome intrusion into the hospital routine. The hospital gates must not be opened too widely. Even children are often victims of this attitude. The writer goes so far as to say that one might well compare the hospital wards of today with the cloisters of the Middle Ages. It is true that attempts are being made to change this structure, but the change is taking place at an unbelievably slow rate. The reader will have to remember that the book is about conditions in England, where tradition is harder to break than in the Netherlands, and where too few hospitals were built after the war, so that the system is lumbered with many outdated institutions. However, its value is that its analysis of the particular situation also sheds a great deal of light on some general problems.

We have seen in the last chapter that the sick man in a primitive culture was treated as the 'other', the outsider, the one who is placed outside the boundaries of the community. Gerda Cohen claims that in the modern hospital, as a result of the old tradition, but also as a result of developments in modern medicine, the sick man is once again, though in a new way, the 'other', the one with rights, without dignity, without status. He is not fully human. Where in the older hospitals he might have been an object of care for the poor or of an old-fashioned rigid nursing system, now in the new hospital there is the danger that he will become the object of increasing specialization. Objectification and isolation of the patient are the hall-marks of the modern hospital.

It is worth putting this book, written with a journalist's flair, alongside a sociological study by Dr J. Winkler Prins, *Huisarts en Patiënt*, a book about the general practitioner and his patient, which devotes some attention to the place of the patient in the modern hospital. As a sociologist, Dr Winkler Prins is primarily interested in the image of the GP in a present-day community, in so far as one can discover this from his relationship to his patients. The psychological aspects of the relationship interest him less. However, the 'role' of the patient in the community is also clearly described. What stands out and is highlighted is the fact that he is 'the other'. Of the patient it is said:

Many of the standards and expectations normal in social intercourse lose their relevance in his case . . . One does not expect the patient to take part as a matter of course in all these social activities (i.e. work, family and societies).

In other words, the sick man is placed outside normal social intercourse. In addition there is already a strong objectifying tendency in the medical examination of the patient: the initiative here lies with the doctor and not with the patient.

During the period of examination, decisiveness and active participation by the patient will often be regarded by the doctor as interference.

Clearly this creates an abnormal relationship.

The author goes on to discuss the hospital and brings out the significance of the isolation of the patient as an important pre-requisite to 'making his behaviour controllable'. While the modern hospital does not carry the process of isolation as far as monasteries, asylums and concentration camps do, a real comparison is nevertheless possible:

The life of a hospital is not only different from normal life in even the smallest detail, but it also has a totalitarian character . . . The authority of the nursing staff over the patient as well as that of the medical staff is of primary importance. The relationship is in a certain sense impersonal . . . This authority structure, in which behaviour is constantly and in every respect controlled, is that in which the child finds himself . . . Almost all authoritative initiative all day lies with the hospital staff.[3]

Clearly Dr Winkler Prins is describing in sociological terms exactly the same situation as Gerda Cohen, a situation of which the hall-marks are the objectification, isolation and the loss of social status of the patient. In the light of this it is not surprising that one of the real dangers of modern hospital life is the so-called hospitalization of the patients – i.e. an excessive hankering after the security, the lack of responsibility and the care provided by the hospital. Not only, as Dr Winkler Prins remarks, do they become 'children', but they dread separation from this 'home' with its father and mother figures. Here we touch on the fascinating problems of the psychology of the sick-bed, to which we will be returning in a later chapter. At this point we simply need to note that the modern hospital, if the description given by Cohen and Winkler Prins is accurate, must harbour within itself a number of tensions. It is out of these very tensions that Cohen's little book is written. She tries systematically to pinpoint where improvements are possible, and all the improvements she suggests are to do with the breaking down of the process of objectification and isolation, and with the consequent increase in the responsibility given to the patient; the hospital needs to become more human. Her basic contention is that it must be possible to treat patients, even in hospital, as fully human beings; in other words, it must be possible to recognize that the patient is not 'other', that his otherness is not essential to him, and with this recognition should come a change in attitudes towards him.

In this situation it will obviously be a considerable help to the patient if he is prepared more carefully than normally happens at present for the experience that awaits him in hospital and particularly for the experience of being treated in the objective way which the development of modern medicine has made almost inevitable. Winkler Prins makes it quite clear that this objectifying process is in the interest of the patient. The GP could play a considerable part in the preparation when discussing entry into hospital with his patient, and this aspect of a patient's needs should be borne in mind in the admission procedures into hospital. One gladly notes that increasing attention is now paid to it.

Recent developments in medical social work in hospitals could possibly contribute indirectly towards the process of preparation, in that social workers, through their contacts with families, may well be able to foster some understanding of the nature of hospital life. I should like to enter at this point an observation about the relationship between the minister and the staff of the medical social department. From a number of conversations with medical social workers in training it has become clear to me that there the respective spheres of their work and that of the minister are bound to overlap at a number of points. It is, therefore, important that the minister should cultivate good relationships not only with the medical and nursing staff but also with the medical social worker. A proper understanding of each other's work and an exchange of information and insights are bound to be fruitful for both sides. One could well argue that the introduction into the hospital of medical social work, with its basic concept that to help people means to encourage and enable them to help themselves, is in itself a sign that there is now a real attempt in the modern hospital to treat a patient not only as object, but as subject. I hope in the next chapter to show that the minister's function, properly exercised, also helps to create a more personal and human approach to the patient.

Another step in the right direction has been the replacement in modern hospitals of the vast wards of earlier days by rooms for one or two patients. This possibly enhances the status and dignity of the patient. Here and there one will find even bolder moves. On a visit to an English psychiatric hospital, for example, I came across an important attempt deliberately to appeal to the healthy, the normal, the fully human capabilities of the patients and to encourage them in a shared responsibility for the life of the hospital by means of open group discussions between the patients, members of the medical staff, nurses and other officials including clergy. Experiments in a similar direction are also taking place in the Netherlands.[4] In one hospital in this country, I know that attempts are made to achieve the same object by giving the patient clearly defined responsibilities for certain aspects of the hospital life – e.g. on the wards. In other hospitals there has been increasing freedom to visit.

We must, therefore, be careful not to see the hospital as a static institution, but rather as one in which far-reaching developments are taking place. The most immediately striking aspects of this development are those which are external, in the medical and organizational fields. Nevertheless, the tensions below the surface to which Cohen draws attention are just as real and just as important for the minister. Below the surface there is quite clearly a development in the direction of breaking down the old-fashioned, closed, strongly hierarchical community and replacing it with a much greater degree of openness and freedom – making it more human. The position of the nursing staff, the relationships between staff grades and between officials, in short the whole social atmosphere, is changing noticeably. This change is bound to influence the place of the patient in the hospital, even though there are special difficulties in his case which may complicate the process of change.

At present the most dramatic developments are taking place in psychiatric institutions. These are often far more modern in their organization than ordinary hospitals. This is clearly because it is precisely through making the whole atmosphere as human and normal as possible that they are able to contribute considerably to the recovery of their patients. There has been a rapid development from the old-fashioned asylum, via the psychiatric hospital or institution, to the psychiatric centre, and this development has been marked by a steady increase in openness and a growing appeal to the patient's sense of responsibility and self-reliance. I am convinced that ordinary hospitals have a great deal to learn from the development. However, as I have already indicated, there are special problems here for a normal hospital. In a normal hospital where most of the patients are physically ill, treatment is obviously very different from that needed in a psychiatric institution: an important contributory factor is that the time spent in hospital is often very much shorter. We have, moreover, already seen Winkler Prins arguing that isolation and objectification are essential elements in the medical treatment of the patient. If this treatment is to be fully effective, then both are essential. Quite clearly he is correct in his argument, but I wonder whether we cannot also approach the whole issue from another direction. It seems to me that there are different factors involved in this process, which are not all equally valid. In order to make clear what is involved here I want to refer back to the previous chapter. We saw there that in a primitive community the sick man was treated in a special manner as 'the other'. We also saw that, with a change in cultural pattern, this sense of otherness seemed to disappear but that traces of it were evident today. Now we find in this chapter a clear impression that within a completely different cultural pattern these traces have not been wiped out, but have rather come to have considerable significance in an entirely new way and within an entirely different framework. This has been pointed out clearly by Cohen. How are we to account for it?

It can no longer be doubted that even in our society the sick man is experienced as 'the other', as one who does not belong to the normal world, as one whose behaviour is not measured by normal standards. In a primitive society the reaction to the sick is above all that of fear; he no longer belongs to the domain of the demons. It seems clear to me that this is still the case today; the sick will awaken feelings of fear. Of course there have been changes in our attitudes towards the sick in many respects. Many diseases can now be cured and they are, therefore, no longer 'dangerous'; consequently the sick are only temporarily 'out' of action. Nevertheless, there is in all sickness a frightening relationship to death, to our final destruction, and we are deeply aware of the fact when faced with incurable diseases. The sick man makes us afraid, because he is on the way out of the normal world towards the *other* world and in a sense has already departed from us. By his very existence he places before us the threat of that nothingness, of that emptiness, which even in our fully occupied existence is always invisibly present.

For society, therefore, the isolation of the patient in a hospital which Winkler Prins argues to be essential to effective medical treatment, is nevertheless also an attempt to evade this confrontation. Its hidden motive is fear. Those who are sick belong in hospitals; they do not belong in the normal life of a modern family. We can see the same tendency to avoid confrontation in the increasing practice of leaving the dead in funeral parlours before burial; the dead also do not belong in our normal world. Thus people evade confrontation with death.

However, it is not only when we are faced with the deeply emotional issue of incurable disease that the sick are experienced as 'the other'. This attitude towards them is equally true at a less disturbing level. The very words 'temporarily out of action' hint at this. We live in a society whose hall-marks are the words 'able' and 'must'. Our place in society is determined by what we are able to do and by the fact that we must work to live. But the sick man is not able, and according to our standards there is no need for him to work. This immediately places him outside the world of normal people and makes him clearly 'the other'. In his fellow-men he will arouse ambivalent feelings: on the one hand they will pity him and surround him with care, but on the other hand they will also feel a little jealous and slightly begrudge him his rest. The sick man must not pretend sickness or misuse his position and, when we are faced with psychosomatic illnesses, it is often difficult to suppress the thought that in some way the sick man has only himself to blame for his illness. In general, people are much more prepared to accept physical illnesses, where the inability to act is quite obvious, than neurotic illnesses, where the physical inability is lacking, and one is therefore not inclined to take the illness quite as seriously.

Through his *not being able* – probably linked for him with the threat of the world of death – the sick man makes a clear appeal to his fellow men. He needs our care. He provides others with the deep satisfaction of being allowed to care for the sick. This caring has two aspects. The sick man asks for our care in his inability; he hopes that we will look after him. This is the aspect of nursing. The other aspect is that of caring, that the sick man will once again become able. He must be enabled to start work again and for that he needs to recover: the patient needs in a sense to be repaired. This is the aspect of medical treatment. You could see a hospital as an extremely well-organized repair-business. Clearly this is increasingly how hospitals are in fact regarded. In the course of the past few decades, the modern hospital has lost the atmosphere of the home, in which you could be ill in peace and to which you could escape from the bustle of family life and where you would be well cared for in the course of therapy. We are beginning to see business features, attention to efficiency. This means that there is less and less regard in the hospital for the *suffering* of the patient. There is less and less understanding in the modern hospital that suffering can be a formative power in a man's life, as Scheler and, following him, Rümke asserted. A German doctor wrote several years ago, perhaps rather exaggeratedly but certainly not without reason, about the 'illness of not being able to be ill' caused by modern medical organization.

We see, then, that the great need to care, to nurse, to treat (repair) is bound up with the life of a hospital. The sick man in his otherness, his inability, makes calls on us which can afford deep satisfaction to us, if we obey. Yet it is precisely at this point that a barrier arises to the kind of radical renewal pleaded for by Cohen. The patient needs to be made as far as possible into a 'controllable object' (Winkler Prins) not only for certain 'repairs' such as operations, but also because our need to care for another can at first only be satisfied if we are allowed to treat him in this way. The modern hospital acquires its distinctive character not only from the progress of medical science and technique, but also from the organization of the *need to care*. One gets the impression that our increased understanding of the psychology of the patient is making us more aware that to care for someone may mean that we try to help him to be as fully human as may be: instead of meeting his childish needs we must also constantly be aware of the adult, who wishes to be treated as adult. Responsible caring implies a double approach to the sick, who on the one hand are in need of warmth, security, and rest, but on the other hand also have the right to think and decide for themselves. To care for another means, therefore, besides seeing him as the object of our care, to want to accompany him on the way to maturity, to see in him the subject who is only truly subject when we give him the opportunity to share responsibility – even in the hospital itself.

These considerations are of decisive importance for the 'role' of the minister in hospital. He stands between staff (medical and nursing) and patient. We notice that, in order to gain some sense of security in an uncertain position, he will often identify himself with the staff and with the patient in turn. It is perhaps possible to see a difference here between the hospital chaplain and clergy visiting members of their congregation or parish.

My impression is that the regular hospital chaplain, living as he does within the pattern of the hospital, is tempted subconsciously to identify himself with the attitude of the staff. Sometimes he joins in regarding the patients as the objects of (pastoral) care. He then sees them as people for whom he is responsible: he wants to speak *to* them, perhaps to educate them, to help them find their place in the hospital, to gain a better attitude towards themselves and life, in short, to 'treat' or manipulate them with the tools of his trade. He sees them lying in bed, and it is this which determines his view of his task. The genuine minister approaches his work differently. He rather sees people (subjects) in front of him and tries to enter into a relationship with them, if that is their desire – he tries only to be there, available: above all he attempts to listen and, where this would be real in their situation, to journey with them for a while in the light of the gospel. Every patient and every situation with which the minister is confronted will then become unique.

The other temptation is that faced by the minister who comes from outside to visit a member of his congregation. Experience has taught us that this man will experience the hospital as threatening: the people in uniform, corridors busy with officials, the stretchers, the doors with their impressive labels, all this makes him unsure of himself. As a result he identifies himself sub-consciously with the person he has come to visit, who has to experience all this in the isolation of being the patient. Sub-consciously he will transfer his fear and uncertainty to the patient, even if outwardly he only appears to show his interest by asking the patient whether he is pleased with the place, whether he is longing to go home, what the doctors say about his condition. In so doing he is not able really to listen to the sick person, because, without knowing it, he only has ears for that which confirms his own uncertainty. There is little chance of beginning to journey together. In order to be helpful in visiting the sick in hospital, the visiting minister must learn to recognize the uncertainty the place arouses in him, and then to use this understanding the better to listen to the patient in *his* uncertainty.

# 3

# The Patient in Hospital

We have seen that in hospital the patient is put in the situation of becoming an *object*, the object of examination, of treatment, of nursing. He lives in a network of related functions in which a large number of people deal with him: the specialist, the radiologist, the hospital analyst, the nursing staff, etc. Yet he himself has virtually little or nothing to do in all this: he has to *let* himself be treated and is entirely dependent on decisions made about him by others. All this tends to make him feel uncertain. Where up to now he has been used to making his own decisions and acting on his own initiative, he suddenly has to entrust himself to a number of people he does not know in an unfamiliar situation, and on these people depends the outcome of his illness, which is already filling him with anxiety. It follows that he will need to be reassured and to find security, even if he does not always express this need clearly. In the face of uncertainty about the outcome of his sickness, he will look to the doctor for reassurance and will seek security against the threat of the whole hospital set-up from the nurse. Clearly, then, both doctor and nurse play key roles in the emotional life of the patient.

One is often left with the impression that childish emotional and behaviour patterns which one had imagined to have been shed long ago, re-emerge. What happens here in the emotional life of the patient is what Freud describes as 'regression', a falling back on earlier patterns, which makes fear and uncertainty easier to cope with. What is called 'hospitalization' is in effect nothing other than such regression. Entry into the foreign world of the hospital is a deeply shaking experience for the patient, which he is not normally able to absorb adequately all at once. Sometimes patients will seek to identify themselves with their new situation in a childish and almost masochistic fashion by an almost abject submission. At other times, in an equally childish reaction, they will stubbornly seek to maintain their links with their own world, through trying to go on working and worrying about it. It normally takes a few days to adjust and strike some balance, but even then the patient's emotional life will tend to be pitched at a lower, more childish level. He then tends to live in a private world, in which doctor and nurse provide the necessary reassurance and security, and in which even members of his own family are experienced as visitors from another, rather distant world. If we try to imagine ourselves in this situation, we will understand that in the process of adjustment to hospital life the patient will experience and have to work through aggressive feelings, without necessarily being aware of what is happening. The minister may well notice that some seem to have endless complaints about the food, their fellow patients, the nurses, etc., while others speak of the hospital in such excessively glowing terms that one suspects that here also there are difficulties in adjusting to their situation. In an absorbing description of the stay of a seriously-ill person in a Parisian hospital, *The Patient*, Georges Simenon describes a patient's relationship to his doctor, who is also a personal friend, a relationship in which aggression is clearly present. The reader would be well advised to study the account in connection with the present chapter.[1] As is often the case, the patient's relationship with the doctor is no less free of aggressive features than the child's relationship with the father. Cohen, too, has drawn attention to this side of hospital life.

Towards the nurse, aggressive feelings will be less to the fore, though every nurse knows that they occasionally become both visible and vocal. By her presence she creates a sense of warmth and security in the threatening atmosphere of the hospital. Simenon's story depicts this significance of the nurse's presence in masterly fashion. However, aggression is present, though it manifests itself in a different way. When aggression cannot be expressed, it will tend to be turned inwards and declare its presence indirectly through self-reproach and guilt feelings. Patients sometimes appear to the nurse to be bowed under excessive guilt feelings and to reproach themselves bitterly for some unkind remark or even an unfriendly thought. Such excessive guilt feelings can also play a role in the patient's relations with his family. The minister will sometimes come across them in conversation with the sick, or when his advice is asked about conflicts between the patient and his family. It is as well that he should be aware of the existence of these childish emotions engendered by the patient's difficulties in adjusting to the hospital situation.

In a study of the patient in hospital, Dr J.J.C.B. Bremer has some thought-provoking comments about this sense of insecurity. He does not deal with the apparent need to work through feelings of aggression, but their existence and the pressures they exert are evident in his observations.[2]

We may nevertheless distinguish certain general aspects of the hospital situation. It is a highly ambivalent atmosphere, at once frightening and fascinating, threatening and reassuring, serving and domineering, saving and wounding. At some point on the way to his sick-bed the patient begins to have to surrender his identity. More than anywhere else in hospital, his body becomes an object, something he possesses. He finds himself being identified with his body, while simultaneously 'separated' from it as it is probed and tested as an object.

He enters an unpredictable situation, in which he feels closely hemmed in. It is not just the incapacity brought upon him by his illness but the whole set-up which hinders him in adjusting . . . The common bond of their illness makes his contact with fellow-patients much easier than is usual for him. The doctor is the personal symbol of the longings which fill his expectations. The nurse is unmistakably his refuge. Of all the members of the hospital staff, it is she in whom the patients confide their joys and sorrows . . . The unpredictable, the unfamiliar in the hospital situation are emphasized through failure to prepare the patient for the things that are going to happen and through the lack of some explanation of all that is done around him and to him.

It needs little imagination to grasp that through illness a man's psychic life is subjected to pressures which are bound to have an effect. Obviously illness makes a man much more dependent than he is used to being. He is dependent on the doctor and on the effectiveness or ineffectiveness of his treatment. He is dependent on others for visits, a cup of tea, his food and drink. Of course it is true that in normal life we are also in a measure dependent on others, that we know the difficult feeling of having to wait on the decisions of others; but we also have great advantages denied to the sick: we arrange our own timetable, we can be productive in our work. Not so the patient; often he is not allowed to work, only to read a little, and he is certainly not master of his time – his meals are at mealtimes, 'lights out' is fixed, he is washed on time, etc. The sense of being passive which the need to lie in bed inactive readily breeds, soon spreads to the whole of his life.

It is not to be overlooked that the care of the sick, in our society, is normally in the hands of women. Inevitably this gives the relationship of the sick to the nursing staff kinship with the mother-child relationship. Like a child the patient has to be washed and tucked up; his food is prepared for him on his plate; sometimes he needs help with drinking. He has to be washed like a child by the nurse, and like a child he is expected regularly to use the bedpan and to 'present' nurse with the results (sometimes with the feeling that it is a present).

Even if the patient himself is reasonably able to resist such pressures through a strong sense of independence, he is still liable to find himself 'wrapped' up in this kind of child relationship by the attitude of members of the nursing staff. This is especially true of older nurses, who tend to scold or praise their patients like children and to encourage or rebuke them in nursery language. It is a role which they have gradually come to play and which has often been of considerable help to them in carrying out their work efficiently. Sometimes we hear of the 'childish behaviour' of the sick. I believe that we describe the psychology of the sick-bed most accurately when we take as our starting-point the fact that illness almost inevitably is accompanied by a return to childish behaviour patterns previously suppressed or overcome, using 'patterns' in a wide sense. Being laid up in bed, constantly dependent, nursed by women, prevented from moving about, which in life is one of the main sources of our sense of independence, and the intangible threat of the whole situation, all combine to produce the 'infantile atmosphere' in which many patients soon find themselves enveloped. One could say that that part of the person whose function it is, through the business of active life, to direct our mental and emotional life becomes weaker and hence allows the more infantile element which lies at the base of all our lives, partly suppressed, partly outgrown, to awaken to the stimulus of a number of associations and to rise to the surface. We should also remember that because of this, many who have not found contentment in the reality of their daily life but, on the contrary, may well have had to wrestle with all sorts of disappointments and frustrations, tend to have a nostalgic longing for the infantile state with the mother's care and protection.

We should distinguish this 'childish behaviour pattern' from a form of regression which is 'biological' rather than 'psychological', noted by the authors of an article on the influence of psychic factors on the appearance and development of tuberculosis of the lungs. They ask:

What tends to happen when someone suddenly falls ill or hears from his doctor that they have found a 'spot' on the lung, so often associated with tuberculosis? The first effect is that the patient withdraws his interest from the world around him and focuses it on himself. This is fundamentally a useful reaction of a psycho-biological nature, which makes the patient prepared to spare himself and to take the steps needed for his recovery. Because of his illness the patient is less able, and because of this reaction less willing, to fulfil the demands which the outer world makes on those in good health. This, moreover, makes him more inclined to follow the directions of doctor and nurse. From another point of view society is making a different set of demands on the patient. It is expected that he will become dependent; he is allowed to be that. He needs more help and he will receive it. This partial relinquishing of the realities of adult life is a regression to an earlier, childish adaptation to life. It is essentially a return to the earlier physiological attitude of childhood, in which the material and emotional needs of a child, not yet able to cope with the outer world on its own, made it similarly dependent upon the care of its parents.[3]

We should note that besides this instinctive withdrawal from the outer world, which one also finds in animals, there is also a regression which is the consequence of pressures surrounding the sick-bed. These two, in the last analysis, influence one another, but they are different in character and need to be distinguished. The word 'regression' is in fact a good term to define the psychic aspect of illness. Freud defined it as 'the return from a higher to a lower stratum of development'. It is a description which does more justice to reality than the description often applied to such behaviour as being 'egocentric'. Egocentricity is a mark of regression, but there is much more to regression than that.

As regression to a stratum of psychic development previously left behind is considered to be an aspect of neurosis, we could therefore speak of a neurosis of the sick-bed. Let us be quite clear that we are not saying that every sick person is neurotic in the sense that he is emotionally sick. As would be the case in any neurosis, we would seek to distinguish between the healthy and the sick parts of his personality even in the 'normal' patient. We would therefore prefer to suggest that the psychic life of the patient oscillates between the twin poles of health and sickness.

We do in fact meet neurotic symptoms in patients, but often we can also appeal to a healthy ego and, as ministers, discuss moral and religious issues with patients. We need, however, to be aware that what we have to say may fall on neurotic ground. Our ministry to the sick will therefore require even greater care and caution than that to the healthy. We speak fruitfully only when the sick person has had an opportunity to speak freely and openly, when he has come to himself, when the necessary 'transference', to use a term coined in psychotherapy, has been established.

What, then, are the psychic phenomena we are likely to observe in the sick and need to understand against this background of ideas? First, we notice that the sick will often lose the *inhibitions* acquired during their upbringing. Life in the ward can sometimes be pretty uninhibited, while at the same time showing signs of excessive prudery. Attacks of jealousy and temper are less easily contained. Often there will be an atmosphere of intimacy which to outsiders sometimes looks 'unhealthy' but which may, sometimes at any rate, be considered healthy in that suppressed feelings are given tongue. Patients will tell one another the most intimate details of their personal lives, so that they will quite often later be ashamed and embarrassed at all they have laid bare. Remarks about the food, the behaviour of fellow patients, the nursing staff, are tossed about with more abandon than one finds outside. On the other hand, people also find it easier to bring themselves to apologize than is normally the case.

In the second place, many patients tend to be *demanding* in a childish and unrealistic way. While it may be too much to say that they expect everyone to be at their beck and call, they nevertheless expect many people to visit them and require that those who look after them should always be friendly and cheerful, however long and arduous the task. I once came across two young wives in hospital from the same village who had compiled a list of all those they expected to pay a visit and, when they failed to come, sent a message via their husbands demanding to know why. Patients find it difficult to grasp the variety of tasks that nurses have to do and how their timetable works, and will therefore make apparently unreasonable requests for glasses of water and other trivial services, or they will keep nurses engaged in unduly long conversations.

Thirdly, we note that patients' behaviour often shows a marked increase in *tenderness*, which is understandable in this connection. This also is the mark of a child and is typical in the sick man. He is readily moved – often to tears. Some passage from a book or story touches him much more deeply than we would normally expect from him. Receiving a letter or some flowers may 'make his day'. He is touchingly grateful to nurse or wife for all she

does for him, in a childish tender way. Often he will talk about
his children and not infrequently will brush away a tear or two.

What is only superficially the opposite is that we will also find
the sick at times *jealous and able to sulk* for long periods. This,
too, is simply another manifestation of a childish behaviour-
pattern. This is very clearly the case in the *tendency to self-pity* –
which is to be found in every sick person. Those with greatest
inner strength will consciously attempt to suppress self-pity,
and where the patient indulges it, it will be with a bad conscience.
He feels himself lonely, which is not quite the same as alone.
There is a feeling of having been deserted unjustly. Even if he
does not complain, one may often tell from the way he lies in bed
or talks that the tendency to self-pity is there. Linked to this
tendency is the sub-conscious desire for attention found in many
patients. Loneliness is banished by the attention the patient
manages to get. The sick are sometimes spoken of as 'naughty',
i.e. they often seek to exaggerate their illness, pain or loneliness
in order to arouse pity, care, in short to gain attention.

Professor Rümke says about hysteria:

The hysteric lives in complete isolation. Many people have at some
stage sensed this loneliness and it drives them perpetually to search for
more. It is this very human urge to communicate which here in dis-
torted form dominates the picture.[4]

This comment on the hysteric can in a lower key be applied
to the sick and makes his so-called 'naughtiness' understandable.

We can say, then, that the experience of being ill produces
certain characteristic effects in the patient. At the same time it
also results in the loss of certain capabilities acquired in the years
of growing maturity. In the language of Freud, the willingness
and ability to face reality seem to disappear. *Wishful thinking*
plays a considerable part in the life of the sick. On the one hand
the patient appears constantly to observe the symptoms of his
illness or to seek confirmation of his fears in the remarks of those
around him, especially the medical staff, and generally seems to
be preparing himself for the worst; yet, on the other hand, one
will have to conclude that he appears to have difficulty in getting

a sound hold on the situation, despite the most luminously objective explanations of the doctors. In the lower strata of his personality he is rejecting an unfavourable diagnosis and indulging in wishful thinking. We are not now talking about the last hours of illness, when there is sometimes a sudden access of clarity and insight, which can bring the relief of talking openly with one's family and with a minister. We are talking here about a patient who is seriously ill but for whom there is no imminent danger of death. I know of instances in which the minister, who was aware of the seriousness of the situation, and wanted to discuss this with the patient, was not even given the chance to speak at all but found himself rejected. The problem of 'speaking the truth' in illness is therefore not only an ethical but also a psychological problem. We must be prepared to find amongst those who are ill people who in childish fashion play hide and seek with truth. We all know how in the child's psyche 'poetry' and 'truth' flow in and out of one another and hence how difficult it is to speak of 'lying' in children.

In the second place, the sick person is normally *not very brave*. Here again we come across an infantile lack of preparedness to accept realities. Men who normally are decisive and well able to give sound advice to others, often react childishly even to the taking of medicine, let alone to following the doctor's prescriptions. Those who are ill also find great difficulty in carrying out the good resolutions they make: work they have set themselves to do usually does not get very far – 'I never got round to it'.

Next we need to consider the process of catharsis, or inner cleansing, which often takes place during illness, though one has to observe, alas, that the results are often not very lasting! In a fine book about 'the art of being ill'[5] a doctor, F. Delhez, writes of the significance of the silent hours for the sick. We believe that he is right, and would say that it is typical that they should assume this significance for those laid low with illness. It is one of the functions of the ego to repress those aspirations arising from the sub-conscious which are unpleasant to itself. There are, however, few people who pass through life without a sub-conscious dissatisfaction with themselves. Their life at home and at work is not what it should be, but they tend to skate over the problem, even though they sub-consciously sense that it is precisely this superficiality which is their great mistake, which prevents them from coming to an inner peace. In sickness the ego, as we have already seen, tends to function less strongly; the many problems and concerns which keep us occupied in our daily life have little hold on us, and hence the desire to be a better person, which has for long sub-consciously been disquieting us, becomes stronger. We want to come to a clear understanding of ourselves, for once to talk seriously about ourselves with someone. We recognize our shortcomings and ask for forgiveness more readily in sickness than in health, which is understandable in the light of what has been said; in so doing, there can come a very wonderful peace to the sick man. He has learnt to see himself more clearly; he has been rid of his disquiet, and he is determined from now on to live a different and better life. Hence sickness can become the occasion of strong feelings of joy and happiness. However, not all are able to sustain these insights when they have recovered. There are examples of people who have definitely been converted in the course of their illness, but it needs to be remembered that conversion in this instance takes place during an 'infantile' phase, when the patterns of inner life are quite other than in normal health. Lasting conversions are, in the estimation of many ministers, exceptional.

We now turn to the discussion of a second series of psychic phenomena. The first point we need to observe at this stage is that illness, as well as bringing pain and discomfort, also provides extensive gratification of certain sub-conscious desires. Hence we notice that many patients seem to be attached to their illness. The infantile situation created by the sick-bed has certain advantages: one is cared for, finds oneself the object of affection and protection; there is no sense of responsibility for the sometimes important decisions that have to be taken; the worries and struggles of daily life have been pushed to one side. Of course there are also the dark sides: the pain, the sense of being deserted;

the suspicion of 'being kept out of it' which can nag away so often at women who have had to hand over their household to another; the feeling of rebellion at the fact that others constantly make decisions about us as a matter of course and treat us 'like a child'; and the gnawing uncertainty about the outcome of our illness. Nevertheless, this in no way removes the fact that the situation of dependence, with all that entails, can also bring satisfaction. Hence we note that despite the often-expressed longing to be well enough to walk again in the room or street, there is also at times a kind of fear of the world of the healthy. I have come across those who, after a long illness when given the chance of recovery through some new treatment, have refused to let themselves be taken to hospital, to the intense amazement of those around them. What we see here is the fear of the freedom and responsibility of normal, adult life, a fear sometimes also encountered in puberty.

Secondly, it needs to be said that in the patient there is also a natural urge towards good health, so that he will work with the doctor in order to become better. Good health, precisely because it affords this freedom and responsibility and also the chance of finding satisfaction in work, certainly has its attraction for the patient. His day-dreams will often circle around all the things he will be able to do and experience when he is well again. Usually, however, it is only certain selected aspects which stimulate the urge towards recovery. Being ill brings such subconscious advantages that it is not health as such which many desire; it is only certain advantages of health which sharpen the desire to see an end to illness. One thinks of the grocer who wanted to stop being ill because he was needed to run his business, or the seaman, for whom the sea-going life meant so much satisfaction. Sometimes the spur is wounded pride, as with the housewife who has to put up with seeing another in control of her domain and even giving her orders. Naturally an important incentive is the distaste for pain, the sight of blood, diarrhoea, and the many torments that accompany illness. The most important force in the nature of things is the desire to escape the threat of

partial or total annihilation inherent in sickness. The will towards
health is often characterized by unwillingness to die or be an
invalid rather than by a positive will to get well. We must therefore conclude that the relationship between the values we attach
to health and sickness is rather more complicated than may at
first glance appear.

The third aspect of a man's reaction we need to study in illness
is how he tends to react to the real possibility of a bad outcome
to his illness, or more acutely, when he is faced with death and
deterioration which he knows to be part of our common lot, as an
imminent experience. He may react in two ways, by accepting the
fact or by rejecting it. *Rejection* may show itself either in an
attempt to ignore the situation or in a neurotic surrender to the
illusion that one is not really all that ill, certainly not so ill as to
be in any serious danger of death. Naturally there is a frequent
change of mood. *Acceptance* of this aspect of one's illness can
likewise show itself in different ways. It can have the character
of resignation to the inevitable, the realization that we will just
have to accept it. It can, on the other hand, be an acceptance in
faith, in the conviction that we are in the hands of God and that
here sickness and death have no final power.

When people find the strength to face illness in a positive way,
we come across an experience which is sometimes described as
'learning the lesson of suffering'. The lesson is this, that, through
such a confrontation and through the distance at which one is
set from daily life, one gains a deeper insight into the relative
values of the various aspects of one's life. In the 'silent hours',
work, family, recreation, the people with whom one has to do,
the way in which one comes to tackle the great issues of life, are
all seen in a new perspective. Here we are touching upon that
catharsis spoken of earlier on.

One of the striking features which emerges from our study
of the difficulties faced in illness is the sick person's need of community. In the regression brought about in his illness he cannot
do without the security provided by father-figures and the safety
afforded by mother-figures; the presence of friends, 'brothers

and sisters', can also be of real importance. He is afraid of being forgotten, of no longer belonging. One could say, in short, that the patient depends upon *the solidarity* of his surroundings with him.

In hospital it is normally the specialist who represents the expert authority to whom the patient entrusts himself. He is regarded sometimes as a comrade, sometimes as a 'father', who thinks and fights on the patient's behalf. A difficulty arises, therefore, when the patient is being sent from one specialist to another: this creates the feeling that nobody knows, that there is no 'father' who really takes his part. It may well be that the registrar in the hospital could play a key role in this situation as the co-ordinating figure at the centre of things who makes the patient feel the object of proper attention. The relationship with the registrar is, however, different from that with the specialist in charge of a patient's case in an important respect. Once the patient is in the hands of the specialist, the registrar loses that 'authority' which in hospital the patient needs above all. On the other hand, there are sides to the patient's relationship with the registrar which are not found in that with the specialist, e.g. the need for advice, clarification, attention. These will be all the more prominent when the patient is also in the hands of a specialist.

In general, therefore, in the emotional life of the sick the doctor plays the role of the comrade-father who cares, knows and advises. In the crisis-situation of the hospital this role is, as it were, split into two: the specialist becomes the one who knows and acts, while the registrar is more the one who gives attention, makes things clear, provides support. He knows the patient and the specialist; he knows the workings of the hospital, so that his very presence already makes the patient's lot more bearable.

The nurse provides this feeling of solidarity in another way. She is more constantly present, the one who cares for the patient, washes him, bandages his wounds, administers pain-killing injections, straightens his bedclothes, gives him the bedpan, deals with feeding; she gives him a friendly nod or smile, at night checks from time to time that he is all right. In all this she is not so much a comrade as the sister-mother figure, who simply by her presence creates a sense of safety, restfulness and security. She does not have to say much, but she will need a ready sympathy and patience.

The need to sense this solidarity also plays a great part in the relationships between patients. They are interested in each other's experiences, cheer one another up or spare one another in considerate ways; they will warn the nurse when something appears to be wrong with a fellow patient. In a way the ward is the 'children's nursery' for the patients where quarrels and jealousies play their part, but where it is also pleasing to be together and pull together, in the house of their parents – the doctors and nurses.

The minister also enters this world with its peculiar network of thoughts and emotions, to fulfil his task. He, too, is used by the patient to answer his need for community and solidarity. Usually his presence is welcome, even though the associations with parting and guilt can make his coming a thing to be feared for some. On the whole, people expect and hope for something from him, and the simple fact of his presence expresses his willingness to be with them. As representative of the church he can bring to some the sense of things treasured and familiar, the more so if he is the minister from the patient's own church or parish, but even the otherwise unknown hospital chaplain can give the impression that here is one prepared to listen, to help a person on the way, one who may show some path or shed light on the confusions and uncertainties of being ill. He is, then, a man who, without obtruding himself, wants for a while to be a companion on the way and one who knows of another 'world' beyond and above this present one.

The sick have to wrestle with all kinds of drastic problems. They have to come to terms with pain, uncertainty, the curtailing of life's opportunities, reflection about their life and the various guilt-feelings that this arouses. They will try to cope with these alone, but usually it proves to be beyond them. Then for the sick comes the need to be allowed to tell someone, to talk quietly, to come to some clearer understanding of it all. It is true that the sick man would like to be helped, to receive guidance, but what is so often lacking is the one who gives him the sense of being listened to properly. The minister is much more than a friend to whom a man can open his heart. He has a task, an 'office'; he is in the service of the gospel. Yet in the ministry to the sick, even more than usual, he will only fulfil his task of pointing men to the gospel, when he has carefully *listened* and given the other to know that he genuinely seeks to be *with* him in solidarity. We can only help the sick when we are ready to accept them in the reality of their situation, without any attempt, conscious or unconscious, to force or reproach them. It is surprising how often the latter happens.

When we try to get a clear picture of the effect the minister has in the patient's situation, we will see that he is one of the few figures in the hospital who help to 'personalize' the situation. For him, the patient is not an 'object under control' but a subject, a fellow human being, admittedly in exceptional circumstances, but nevertheless in a situation in which he needs to be encouraged to be human, in which he requires the chance to talk about his illness and frustrations, to understand them more clearly, to see them set in the light of the gospel. When his relationship with the patient is sound, the minister will appeal to the adult, mature part of him. The minister will be fully aware of the psychological implications of regression in the sick, but in his dealings with the patient he will seek to guide him at a level above that to which he has regressed.

Clearly this aspect of the pastoral ministry causes problems in the actual setting of the hospital. Of particular importance is the difficulty the minister faces in that, on the one hand, he is expected to identify himself with the hospital, i.e. feel 'at home' in it and not a stranger, ill at ease, while on the other hand his task requires that he keep a certain distance. I want to discuss this situation in some detail, as it raises considerable practical problems in exercising a hospital ministry.

We can start from the idea quoted in the Preface, that the minister in hospital is an 'alien body', a figure who is not 'at home' there. It is necessary, however, to distinguish between two levels in this situation. On one level, that of his task and function, the minister is of necessity a 'foreigner'. The hospital is a therapeutic institution for which the medical staff are responsible and in which everything is geared to treating and curing the patients. The minister has a different commission; he does not really belong to the 'staff'. It may be that he attends staff meetings and there in his pastoral capacity plays a consultative role; nevertheless, his responsibility is other than that of the medical and nursing staffs. His *role* is not in the area of treatment or nursing care. And yet he cannot remain a foreigner in practice. Far from it: if he is to carry out his task properly, he will need to be integrated in some way. He will need to be known and acknowledged, to be reckoned with, to be given a place as colleague, fellow-worker, perhaps as friend. It must be made possible and easy for him to exercise his ministry. From another point of view it needs to be said that he himself will have to seek and strive to build up a relationship which is integral to the life of the hospital. Where he tries to be co-operative in his turn, he will find himself more readily accepted. This needs to be emphasized, because experience shows that clergy in this respect are often unhelpful, whatever the reason may be.

We will only make progress in understanding this situation if we recognize that the hospital, for the minister too, is primarily a medical institution, concerned with the tasks of diagnosis, treatment and nursing. In principle, the minister's relationship to this institution is the same as that of the women running the library, the hairdresser and others whose work may well be of importance to the patients, perhaps even necessary, but who are not directly concerned with the proper task of the hospital. He will therefore have to find a vacant spot for himself, and while he may certainly count on co-operation from the staff, he can in no way 'reserve' this spot. If the patient should be needed for an operation or for tests, then he has no claim because he had arranged to talk with him at this time. His dress will also mark the minister out as a stranger in principle: by contrast to all other members of the staff he does not wear appropriate hospital uniform. I take it that no one reading this has ever encountered a hospital chaplain dressed in a white coat.

When we grasp the essentials of this situation, we can see that the minister in his hospital ministry is faced with a number of problems which, perhaps with help from the staff, he will have to solve. We have already mentioned the sense of uncertainty that can come over him in hospital. It is inevitable that he should be uncertain on entering this institution, uncertain of his place (Will people be helpful? To whom should he apply?) and uncertain of his role (What do the doctor and nurses discuss with 'his' patient and what is he to discuss? Does he really understand this new world in which the patient has landed sufficiently to give him support?). Behind this there may well be a profounder uncertainty. The doctors seem to have acquired an objective approach towards the great problems of suffering and death; they appear to be familiar with them, while the minister is uncertain in such 'boundary situations', aware of the uncertainty present in his own faith, and yet knowing that for him professionalism would be an escape from reality. The sick can only be helped by him if his contact is not professional but personal.

There is a further uncertainty which we touched on above. The minister who comes from outside the hospital finds difficulty in inwardly accepting this world with all its suffering on the one hand and its sophisticated technical equipment on the other. The threat posed by the modern hospital sometimes affects him even more than the patient, who at least has the security of knowing that he is 'in good hands'. Often this uncertainty will be accompanied by a sense of competition with the medical staff, who matter so much more now to the patient than he – a feeling reciprocated by some doctors – and this makes it difficult to work together. It is noticeable how little objective, professional contact there is between doctors and clergy, even outside hospital life. Many clergy also find themselves uncertain, because they have not yet realized that a good working relationship with the nursing staff, especially the ward sister, is important. They will often ignore the nurses. Even when a minister has recognized their importance, he will still have that feeling experienced on seeking entry to the company director via the secretary: you feel you are being subjected to scrutiny by someone female and 'lower down'. Very often his assessment of the hospital hierarchy is at sea, and hence he fails to realize that the staff nurse or sister is his 'hostess' and wishes to be recognized, and that in fact she has far more executive power than he is aware of.

This sense of uncertainty is in effect part of the wider problem of the place and identity of the clergy in modern society. It is, however, the considered opinion of those engaged in clinical training courses in hospitals that younger clergy find it peculiarly difficult to believe in their pastoral identity in the hospital setting, alongside doctors and nurses. The solution to this will only be found on the one hand in a deeper awareness of one's pastoral ministry, to which such courses make a significant contribution, and on the other in a more open working identification with the hospital. The minister must seek to make himself at home, to enjoy the contacts made in the course of his work, and in consequence to take part in the social life of the hospital. He has to succeed in striking a balance between distance and identification.

Finally, some observations about the way in which the hospital staff may see the clergy. Often the minister is not aware of the image others have of him. The staff will often find his presence as an alien body irritating and inconvenient. They will often find him authoritarian, because he does not know his place and tends to go his own way. He can irritate the nursing staff by seeking access to patients without regard to convenience, thus upsetting the 'family' routine. Sweet vengeance, then, for the nurse to make fun of him – as she does at times of the medical men. The medical staff do not come across the minister to the same extent, but in the structure of the hospital he can represent a threat to them also. He talks with the patients. What about?

Does he tend to make them more anxious or does he have a quietening influence? It is so difficult to get a clear picture of his work and his identity. This is, of course, truer of the visiting minister, but the hospital chaplain will need to be aware of the situation, too.

# 4

# Some Pastoral Problems in Hospital

*Faith and Illness*

Every minister knows that there can be a powerful interaction between a man's faith and his illness. A number would hold that illness can be overcome and cured by faith. Others, who have reservations about this view, would nevertheless appeal to the sick man's faith to help him rise above and cope with his illness. In this chapter we want to explore another side of this interaction, the effect that a man's illness can have on his faith. That a man's faith is affected by illness is clear, and, although there is little research on which to base one's observations, we hope to make some of the effects of this interaction which the minister is likely to meet in his ministry more easily understood.

We all know how sickness can undermine faith. This will show itself sometimes in loss of heart, sometimes in rebelliousness, sometimes in a dull indifference. Sometimes the reverse happens: through his sickness a man comes to faith or finds his faith deepened. He then senses a call to use his illness and work through it to some purpose; he believes himself to be safe despite all, and he can be thankful for the new understanding of life to which his sick-bed has brought him. If we are to understand this interaction between illness and faith, we need to start from the realization that illness is a deeply frustrating experience in a man's life. Where the illness is at all serious, it disrupts plans made in his work, for holidays, for the many things he likes to do. Moreover the body, which in time of health is subject to his wishes as a matter of course, is suddenly out of control. It is no longer his to decide what he will or will not do; instead he finds himself dependent on the decisions of doctors, nurses, analysts and the numerous other members of the hospital staff. And in the midst of all this he is often prey to gnawing doubts about the nature and outcome of his illness.

When we are ill, therefore, we will have to find some way of living with this frustration, of working through it, of weaving it somehow into the pattern of our lives. Put in another way, it means that through illness our inner being is probed and tested to show whether we possess sufficient reserves of inner strength to accept and digest such frustration.

The psychologist has shown that we react to frustration in different ways. Sometimes we react in infantile ways, at others in a realistic and adult fashion. Anyone who has had dealings with the sick or been seriously ill will be aware of both reactions. A reaction is infantile when, because we are not strong enough squarely to face the seriousness of the situation, we try to avert its threat by bringing into play some defence-mechanism, e.g. by convincing ourselves that the illness is not really serious. Anna Freud, in her admirably clear book *The Ego and the Mechanisms of Defence*,[1] has described such defence-mechanisms and shown how readily we avail ourselves of this way of ignoring any threatening or frightening reality. We then tend to fall back on a mechanism which a child, whose inner ego is still weak, uses to cope with the world. We must therefore take care not to give the word 'infantile' disparaging overtones. The power to ignore reality is a mighty force, which has spared many sufferers weeks of agony. Very often, moreover, a process of adjustment is taking place behind this denial of reality, in which the ego is gradually learning to accept the situation and ultimately discovers the relief of being able to discuss it sensibly with doctor, minister and family.

Another infantile reaction one often meets in this ministry lies in the question, What have I done to deserve this? Here the sick man experiences his frustration as unfair, as an injustice. His suffering is seen as a kind of unreasonable punishment. This sense of being punished often summons up deep and disturbing emotions – probably connected with childhood experiences. Sometimes there is a feeling of protest, of grievance at the injustice of it all. Others feel that somehow they have deserved such punishment; many people have this sub-conscious need to be punished. When, therefore, the sick man asks why he has 'deserved' this, the minister will need to listen carefully to distinguish whether he is uttering a protest or asking for help in being purged of his guilt-feelings.

I want to argue that both the need to protest and the search for guilt betoken a lack of faith in the face of illness. We have learned from Freud to recognize how often at critical moments in our life we tend to fall back into childish patterns of emotion and behaviour. Let it be said at once that he considers religion to be always such a regression. The child, according to him, needs the support and protection of its father and therefore creates a Father-God. I am convinced that Freud's theory simply does not do justice to religious experience as a whole; there are adult and mature forms of religion. Nevertheless, it is undeniable that we do also meet such infantile religious reactions. The two reactions under discussion here are such. In the frustrations occasioned by his illness, the sick man regresses to an infantile attitude towards the father: from him he expects protection against his frustrations and, when this is not forthcoming, he either reproaches his father for his lack of love or, feeling guilty because of his aggressive feelings towards the father, expects this punishment from him. Such an attitude is obviously not a mature faith, and the concept of God here is also highly immature. We are dealing with a neurotic faith which is really unbelief. Few will dispute the conclusion that the reaction in which the sick person denies the seriousness of his illness is one which betokens lack of faith, unbelief. Where there is faith, there will be a willingness to face the situation. I would even go so far as to say that an infantile reaction, which springs from the weakness of the ego, is the opposite of faith. Wherever faith is genuine, reality will not be avoided.

We recognize, then, that there can be an infantile, immature reaction to illness. Others who are ill react otherwise, realistically and in a matter-of-fact way. Here, too, reactions will be various. First, illness may be accepted and experienced as simply part of our life, something which is as likely to happen to oneself as it is to other people. It is to be accepted as one of the unavoidable facts of life, an experience everyone ought to expect to face at some time. Of course, there are things that can and ought to be done with illness, but we certainly should not ask what we have done to deserve it. That is a pointless question. Another reaction is that of the person who experiences his illness, like other events in life, as a challenge to his ability to cope with the situation adequately. He allows the fact of his illness to enter openly into his awareness instead of seeking to shut it out and tries – in psychological terms – to integrate this experience into his life. This may happen in several ways. One may hear some say that it is good for them to find time for 'peace' and 'quiet': the routine and rush of normal life is in danger of cutting them off from aspects of life they feel to be important. Hence a sick person may talk about 'lessons learnt' on his sick-bed; he finds that he now sees his work, his relationships, himself, his whole life in a new light. In general this need in some way to 'make use of' one's time of illness is to be found in a number of those who are ill. Max Scheler and Karl Jaspers have often in their writings drawn attention to the formative, creative power of suffering. Scheler argues that it is only through suffering that man breaks through to a profounder level of life and Jaspers that man, in order to become truly human, needs to pass through 'boundary situations' such as the experience of suffering.

Clearly this comes near to what one may characterize as a 'believing' acceptance of illness: his illness is accepted by the one who is sick because in it he can sense some meaning; he has faith. Acceptance becomes explicitly a matter of faith when he bases it on his relationship to God. In the pastoral ministry we hear this acceptance in faith expressed in different ways. One person will speak of God's guidance throughout his life

and the faith that he will lead in illness also; another sees in his sickness a call from God to some task, maybe the task of being a 'good neighbour' even here. A third may have the deep conviction that God knows his needs and is close to him. Yet another will sense in his life the unfolding of God's purpose in which suffering also plays its part; suffering can bring to us a deeper grasp of God's purpose in life. Again, there is the question asked by Job: 'Shall we receive good at the hand of God and shall we not receive evil?' All these are ways of saying that it is the sick man's relationship to God which enables him to accept his illness. Naturally the question arises whether there is not as much a running away in this acceptance in faith as in the denial of the illness or in the questions about 'deserving it'. Freud, as we have already said, sees religion as a neurotic regression to infantile patterns, precisely in the experience of suffering, because it gives one the illusion that 'Father' still cares: in fact 'Father' is not there, but is the product of our childish need for protection and help. Clearly it is quite possible that there is a flight from reality behind some of the kinds of believing responses mentioned above. We have already admitted this. The sick person in that case accepts the situation, because the illusion of a caring 'Father' opens up the possibility of finding a different need met, the need to be loved, in the same sort of way that a child may bear the pain inflicted by the dentist because mother is in the room to comfort him.

I am, however, convinced that Freud's contention that there is no such thing as an adult, mature faith just will not stand up to the facts of experience. We can in fact argue that a realistic, mature acceptance of suffering betokens a measure of faith. This is a contention also made by those followers of Freud who want to ascribe to religion a positive value in the life of man, the best known of whom are Fromm and Erikson.

We have to distinguish, then, between a spurious faith which encourages one to avoid an objective acceptance of reality only by making it bearable, and a genuine faith which leads one to and sustains one in such an acceptance, and through it brings one to the discovery of life at a new depth. If we now ask what influence a man's illness can have on his faith, we can see that there are two possibilities. The first is that his faith stands the test of this experience and is sometimes deepened by it. Every minister will know some such people. If he is realistic, he will be aware of the possibility that people like this may try to use their faith in God to escape the truth about their illness. The minister will need to make Freud's realism his own. All the same, he will not see all faith as an escape, a flight from reality. Sickness can serve to bring to light the real inner strength of a man to cope with reality in all its harshness, however much that reality has deprived him of. We are looking, then, for an acceptance which springs from a certain attitude towards the reality of our existence. It is an attitude which has the power time and again to surmount frustration, because one finds in the experience of this reality something positive. The reality is always *meaningful* and *satisfies*, not in the biological-instinctual sense which the word has in Freud, but in the sense of inner contentment. To believe in, to have faith in reality, is in this sense to be satisfied through it; it is, through it, to grow to a mature, full humanness, through it to find a way of life which is characterized by such words as service, a sense of mission, altruism, freedom, tolerance, dedication, etc. A mature belief in God is one which sets a man free to walk this way. The fact is that it is in this sort of way that we see some who are sick grow in maturity through their sickness. Their faith is tested, but in the testing is deepened and strengthened.

The other possibility is, of course, the opposite of this: we know those who through suffering lose their faith. They engage in a futile rebellion, they feel cheated, they cannot wrestle through to any meaning in it all, they begin to complain, they cannot keep up fruitful relationships with their fellows so that there is no chance of consideration for others, of sympathy, of thinking and feeling things through with others; they feel themselves finally alone and utterly cut off. We can understand this reaction if we recognize that there are people who before they were tested by illness were already using their faith to escape reality, even then making infantile demands on God and filled with immature expectations about him.

Fromm has pointed out in his *Psychoanalysis and Religion* how much faith in the first and proper sense Freud himself had, despite his sharply sceptical approach to religion. His manner of life, his work, the way in which he accepted the frustrations which he was certainly not spared, all point to a considerable faith in reality.

I find the drift of my meaning beautifully captured in a passage from a book by France Pastorelli. Out of her own experience of living for years with a serious heart-disease, she writes:

Yet to discover that a crippled life may still be truly rich is not learnt in a day. It is the fruit of a hard and long schooling . . . I do not always want to ponder my own sorrows; open my heart, O Lord, to those of others . . . My own lot, too, I must judge fairly, and recognize that, however much I may be deprived of, yet my life has known times of deeply moving joy and that my illness has left many rich experiences to be explored . . . Do you know the worst agony of those who are sick? It is the feeling that you have nothing left to offer to those around you; worse still, that you become a burden to them. Yet the truth is that you are only really useless when you cease to want to be of use . . . If 'resignation' means that you give up when you see the ideals of your life slip away, and that you must silence the urge to see the powers hidden within you grow into full bloom . . . then I must admit that I have never been resigned. Far from it: thought that the talents, in the biblical sense of the word, which I had received might have proved useful, had I been well, grew ever stronger, as the hope of healing grew less. And yet I found I could accept the sacrifices asked of me with courage, even though the hurt ran deep. I clung to those things which remained standing in the storm, to the possibilities still left to me, whose priceless value I understood only too well . . . This is the meaning of suffering: in the very hardest of trials it was as if a quiet strength flowed from me to those around. I became aware of the bond which binds souls together, of the ability to pass on spiritual values, of that all-embracing love which makes us living branches of one tree, which the church calls 'the communion of the saints' . . . Do you know when I feel the cold hand of death? It is not in the moments of pain and extreme affliction; these only disturb us because they open up a world of unknown values; no, not in these, but when I contemplate that restless, hunted world in which there seems to be no more point to living than that marked by 'dynamic' and 'existential', when I see hordes hunting like hungry wolves for a satisfaction in life which is in reality no less than a spiritual death, without any genuine culture, without self-awareness . . . The purging of the soul is a mercy vouchsafed to few . . . and to us who are sick falls the painful privilege of finding that our sufferings can become the flame which burns away the dross in our soul.[2]

For those engaged in the pastoral ministry in an hospital it is important to recognize that very few people will discuss their lot with the self-awareness shown by France Pastorelli. She has the ability so to express the problems of her ill-health that these very personal insights can nevertheless be grasped by others. She is able to observe and contemplate her suffering. Those patients whom the minister meets may also need to discuss their condition in general terms – illness provides the time to think – but normally they are wrestling with specific problems and it is these they wish to talk over with him. They are often faced with problems and worries about home, wife and children, or sometimes about work, as well as those about their illness. In a sense they appear to experience their whole lives in a different way. They tend to see their responsibilities more clearly, to feel their shortcomings more acutely, and to work away at their worries rather than to dismiss them. It may well be that during a time of sickness many of the questions and problems one is able to push to one side and run away from in the routine and business of daily life now clamour for attention and can no longer be ignored, as there is plenty of time to think. It may also be that we have here an aspect of 'regression', the desire for an inner purifying we have mentioned earlier.

Sometimes it is the way in which he finds himself facing his illness that gives a man a clearer insight into himself and the shortcomings of his faith: he may then want to talk about his fears, his lack of perseverance or his difficulties in prayer. What is here asked of the minister is therefore not a general discussion about life or belief, but help in understanding and coping with concrete problems. In such a case the minister may well sense, sometimes without being fully aware of it, an element of infantile regression; he may feel that the patient is wrestling here with questions with which he would not normally be bothered, a feeling often shared by the doctors and nurses. There is then the temptation not to take such questions seriously, to dismiss them somewhat airily and to encourage the patient to do likewise by direct suggestion.

Of course there will be times when this is exactly the proper thing to do. In that case one is helping the patient to play down his worries and by suggestion to suppress them, thus strengthening his ego. We need, however, to be very careful. Playing down, making trivial, can be dangerous; for it may well be that the patient is simply not able to suppress his worries and will then, when we have left, feel the more isolated, guilty of failure or rebellious.

I sometimes feel that it is precisely the minister's task to take a man seriously, even when his reactions are somewhat infantile – an approach contrary to that adopted by many on the hospital staff. That means that he must accept the man as he is and listen to him. Naturally this is not always the best course. The minister must learn to detect when he is being used and trapped by the patient and avoid this. Nevertheless he is in principle the one who is not 'treating' the patient – remote, from afar – but the one who seeks to draw near and then to journey with him. It is through this joint looking at and bearing of worries and problems that the patient is enabled to grow out of infantile reactions, to face them in a more mature way and to work through them more objectively. Often, in talking over immediate concrete problems, deeper, more personal problems come to the surface, and the opportunity to face them and talk about them to another can be of immense value. It is the sort of discovery we cannot make on our own. We need another; to be that other is part of the minister's task. I remember, for example, the man who began by admitting to the minister his fear in the face of a drastic operation and then, when he found in him an understanding and sympathetic listener, took courage to confess that his fear was bound up with the fact that he had never told his wife that he had had an affair with another woman and a child had been born from it. At first he had tried to give the minister the impression that his fear sprang from lack of faith, but the minister, able to *listen* carefully, had sensed other causes and had refused to enter into the religious problems.

Let me say again that there are cases in which one may best help the patient by authoritative suggestion, but this is only proper when the minister has *listened* with the utmost care and has sensed that it really is what the patient needs, rather than someone to help him see more clearly. Some ministers are endowed with a natural sensitivity, but they are exceptional. A sound training in understanding human relationships – e.g. the 'sensitivity-training' aspect of the clinical training in which an increasing number of clergy now take part – should be compulsory for all those preparing to enter the ministry. It should be clear, then, that I am wholly opposed to bringing pressure to bear upon the patient. Some years ago, Osborne gained a reputation through the way in which he proved able by mass-suggestion to induce belief and subsequent 'healing' in those who were sick. He even went so far as to state that those not so healed were guilty of unbelief. This kind of healing has all the characteristics and consequences, e.g. impermanence, of a magical, of infantile appeal. Healing through prayer must be deemed a dangerous matter not only from a medical but also from a pastoral point of view.

### Suffering and Death

A vast literature has collected around the problems of suffering and death. In this book we are discussing them in the special setting of the hospital. This setting places them in a special light. Aspects of the problem which play little part in the home assume great significance in the hospital. This is, first, because the modern hospital with its vast technical resources appears constantly to open up new possibilities of cure; and, secondly, because the patient in hospital has to cope with the problems of suffering and death on his own without the support of those whom he loves and trusts. I believe that there is another factor of importance: suffering and death appear to be experienced in a different way. It seems that the vast changes which have taken place in our culture have brought a change in attitude towards suffering and death in their train. There is as yet no clear picture of this change, but there are indications of it. Let me point out some.

In the past the chief accent in man's attitude towards suffering and death lay on the necessity and possibility of accepting them. They were seen as inevitable aspects of a man's life, which could seldom be prevented. But besides this one was aware of another reality which could be attained through suffering. We have already seen the views of Scheler and Jaspers. H. C. Rümke, in a lecture given in 1933 on 'Developmental Psychology and Psychotherapy',[3] aligned himself with these two thinkers and described the possibility as follows:

All understanding is grounded in suffering, and the higher reaches of understanding are only gained through deeper suffering. If this profound saying of Scheler's contains truth – and who would dare maintain that any other way to rich and deeper understanding is to be found than that which leads through the dark corridors of suffering – then one of the conditions of full development must be the ability to suffer . . . Where suffering can on the one hand bring us to a profound understanding and experience of *being*, it can also unfold its full life-destroying power when it comes upon one too weak to face it.

Others in the past have been aware of a reality which transcended suffering and death, as witness a number of our hymns. Yet it is interesting to note that in the new hymnbook of the Nederlandse Protestantenbond, published in 1944, there are no new hymns on the themes of death and everlasting life.

Another indication is that the sick visits of the clergy are gradually changing in character. Originally a visit was understood as a comforting of the sick, i.e. by opening to him other perspectives than those of earth, by preparing him for the inevitable end, a view which is clearly connected with the scant chance of recovery for those who were seriously ill. This character is fading.  Other aims are now present: to help the sick maintain a sense of belonging to the community in a boundary situation, to assist him in coping with his sickness in faith, to encourage him to learn to live at a deeper level. On the Roman Catholic side there has been a corresponding change in the meaning of Extreme Unction: this sacrament was once regarded as the sacrament of the dying; now it is called 'The Anointing of the Sick', and is much less concerned with death.

Clearly, then, we are witnessing the growth of a changing attitude towards suffering and death. The change lies in the gradual move away from *acceptance*. People know and therefore expect that a great deal more can now be done about disease and consequently about the prevention of death than formerly: the number of incurable diseases is shrinking. Increasingly the right to live and to live happily is regarded as one of the basic rights of men. Hence we are more likely to rebel against suffering and death than to accept them as inevitable constituents of our existence. We must add to this that the concept of the loving Father who awaits us, often to be found in older hymns, is fading. We find this clearly argued in, for example, a book by one of the 'death of God' theologians, William Hamilton – *The New Essence of Christianity*.[4] We can, however, trace intimations to earlier thinkers; Bonhoeffer in his letters written from prison in the Second World War, and even Barth's theology after the First War must be reckoned a factor in this development.

The modern hospital is one of the places in our society in which this new climate is clearly to the fore. For that reason I want to examine it more closely. The new development is obviously of fundamental importance for the minister working in a hospital. If he is not aware of the fact that he is working in a climate very different from that in which his predecessors, maybe by only a few decades, worked, he will be unable to assess his place and role properly.

When modern literature explores the thoughts and feelings of our present-day world, we find modern man facing suffering, not with submissive acceptance but with open rebellion. Durieux, the doctor in the now classic novel by Camus, *The Plague*, typifies this rebellion. He protests and does battle against suffering; he finds it meaningless and cannot therefore accept it; at most he can meet it with resignation. For many people today the whole catalogue of woes, natural disasters, wars, congenital defects, the failure of human relationships, both in marriage and at work, incurable diseases, are all no longer something to be endured as part of our human lot, the bad that goes with the good things of life. They see them rather as an absurd side of human life, unreasonable, brutish, 'a shame', things to which you can never resign yourself as a human being, things against which you will find yourself in eternal revolt. One can find this mood well interpreted both in Camus and in many other modern authors. Do we not also have to admit that thoughts such as these also reflect our own attitude and that of our friends?

There is, moreover, the fact that modern technology has made the man of today tackle any obstacle or setback differently. One American has put it this way: 'What is difficult we do today: the impossible takes a little longer.' Suffering, especially illness, is then seen as a challenge, something over which we men must and will be able to demonstrate our power. As men we are powerful or perhaps – the other extreme – (until now) powerless. These are the two poles which determine the attitude of many people. They exclude firmly the old posture of acceptance, of acknowledging given limits to our existence. The new concept of God mentioned above fits well in this climate. In some famous pages from *Letters and Papers from Prison*, Bonhoeffer contrasts with the almighty, sustaining Father God of former times the God who is God precisely in his weakness. He writes: 'God lets himself be pushed out of the world on to the cross. He is weak and powerless in the world, and that is precisely the way, the only way, in which he is with us and helps us'. He goes on to say that we live in a world whose progress is an opening up of 'a way of sweeping the decks for the God of the Bible, who wins power and space in the world by his weakness'.[5]

The changes which have taken place have as yet been scantily studied. But we are well aware of this change in the spiritual climate since the war. We may, for example, recognize it in the changed content of the concept of the tragic. H. J. Heering defines the tragic element in Greek tragedy as being dominated by 'the tension between freedom and necessity',[6] but in this other climate the accent in tragedy falls on the contrast between the vast possibilities open to us and the powerlessness of men in essential points. When, as in a heart-transplant, our technology fails us, we call it tragic. I have already pointed out that the modern hospital is one of the places in our world where this new climate is found. The great advances in techniques and the new possibilities that they open up are fully obvious here; yet, at the same time, the cry of human loneliness and of powerless protest is also heard more clearly. It is perhaps because of this that people in hospital, including the non-religious, will often welcome contact with the clergy.

This has certain consequences for pastoral ministry. It seems to me that the minister must be prepared not to fall back on traditional forms but to try simply *to be there*, to show his solidarity with man in his sickness. One patient who had for several weeks lain seriously ill, described the minister who visited him a few times as 'a man of God'. Perhaps we may say that the *minister* in hospital is a symbolic figure, a man who represents God, makes God present. Furthermore, he does this by calling to one's mind the powerless God of Bonhoeffer who in his powerlessness is with us in the modern hospital, where the sick live in the world of the powerful doctors.

When we are ill our suffering is closely bound up with thoughts of death. In a fine passage in his *Church Dogmatics*, Karl Barth speaks of illness as 'the forerunner and messenger of death'.[7] What, then, can we say of death in the modern hospital, and what pastoral ministry can be exercised here?

Death and the many important pastoral problems faced in dying have been studied much more closely than have suffering and illness. Here, too, we may detect a shift in attitude: there are even 'modern' theories about death. And yet much is unclear. Death is a subject about which much has been thought and written by people representing different academic disciplines. Philosophers have always been interested in it, biologists have studied it, and in the last few years some significant thinking has come from the psychiatrists. Poets past and present have pondered it often. This is not the place to discuss these various points of view. Our aim is to shed as much light as possible from the insights gained from pastoral psychology on the pastoral ministry to the dying, but in so doing we will from time to time make use of insights gained in these other fields.

Let us first note two aspects which, to judge from many funeral sermons and orations, used at one time to play a considerable part in the experience of death. These are views which can still often be met today. There is no hard and fast line between past and present, only a fluid transition. It would perhaps be more accurate to speak of fantasies rather than of views. Around the experience of death people weave all manner of fantasies which show what stance one tries to take towards it, what one expects from it.

First, we meet the fantasy of *homecoming and finding peace*. Our hymns speak of our 'homeland', of 'our abode in the kingdom of blessedness', of an 'eternal home', of 'a city of peace which awaits me at the end of my strife'. Such examples can be multiplied. Expressions such as 'to find rest in the Father's home' (clearly with the accent on the motherly aspects of it) are often found in religious language. In the Old Testament we read of 'being gathered to our fathers'. In general, it is noticeable how often in funeral addresses there is talk of 'resting and peace'.

Secondly, we find in certain circles the concept of *judgment after death* looming large. In and beyond death people expect in this religious fantasy to find the punishing Father, who at our 'homecoming' awaits us with a demand that we give account of our lives. Here a certain strand of belief, i.e. that we constantly stand under the judgment of God and are at all times responsible to him, has been projected to the end of life. In my thesis *On Being Ill*, I came to the conclusion, based on research, that this 'projection' comes into being through a link-up of the fear of death with the notion of judgment.

I have employed the word 'fantasy' deliberately, in order to make clear that our reactions towards the reality of death spring from deeper layers of our inner life. I have therefore used the language of psycho-analysis. One could also have described it another way. In the face of death, the more primitive and primal reactions are aroused and thrown up in a man. He tends to regress to deeper-lying levels of experience. In such fantasies the sub-conscious comes into play. Such sub-conscious fantasy is to be found not only in the words used in funerals, but also in the variety of customs which have grown up around them. The scattering of the ashes after cremation points to a longing to be reunited with the all-embracing universe; the maternal origin is even clearer in burial, the committal 'to the bosom of the earth'. Probably the custom of burning the dead also originally had this significance. Another noticeable 'fantasy' is that we shall be reunited, especially with those close to us.

I believe that we can also see such fantasies at work in the attitudes we take up towards the dying. Those destined to remain behind appear to feel responsible for the one who is dying; they want to care for him, above all not to leave him alone. He needs our help. After all, is he not like a child who needs to draw strength from the 'bosom' of the family – how strongly we sense our belonging together as a family, when we are faced with death – and from the hand which firmly holds him? It is almost as if death is experienced as the mother or father who brings us together, as if it really is felt as the door to the Father's home, to our origin. In the presence of death we suddenly find ourselves brothers and sisters.

In thinking through the problems faced in the experience of death it is important to recognize that genuine emotions, such as fear in the face of death, are not present in our lives from the beginning. First traces of these are not found until the Oedipal stage is reached. The small child has no fear of death. On the contrary. Almost every parent will know how a child's curiosity will draw him right to the edge of the water in which his friend was drowned and, so he was told, thus went to heaven. The Oedipal stage in the child's development is that period in which, for the boy, the mother is the one for whom one longs, to whom one wants to return, the one who guarantees rest and security, the one who loves, while the father, though also the ideal whom one positively admires, nevertheless represents the aspects of punishment and threat.

Many are of the opinion that the problems experienced in facing death are intimately connected with these emotional problems. On the one hand, we find the longing for the peace of death; on the other, the fear of the threatening man with the scythe. Does the scythe arouse fears of castration, fears found in the Oedipal stage? It is probably true that there is a connection between experience of death and Oedipal emotions and that this affects the problems we face in dying, but we need to differentiate further and ask whether there are not other aspects which need to be taken into account.

I have the impression that there are some new aspects emerging in modern society, whose relationship to one another has not yet been studied sufficiently to indicate a clear pattern. I will therefore indicate and discuss them briefly in random order.

(a) When talking about death there is an increasing tendency to see it objectively as the rounding off of life. This is not, of course, entirely new: we have always been able so to value death when it has come at the end of a full and long life. Nevertheless, people died much younger in the past; the average age was much lower, so that one was much more often faced with death as the untimely cutting off of an unfulfilled life.

(b) It has been observed that the experience of dying is not always the same in every phase of life. Little research has so far been done on this, but even on the basis of fairly superficial observations we can say that a child has an experience of death different from that of adults, and also that one's feelings change on growing older, so that death is faced with a certain acquiescence and some times even desired.

(*c*) A new aspect in the present-day situation is created by Freud's concept of the death instinct. Even though by no means all his disciples accept this theory, it nevertheless plays a large part in debate, so that we find it discussed and defended in all manner of modern publications, which would make profitable reading for clergy. One thinks, for example, of Karl Menninger's *Man Against Himself*[8] or K. R. Eissler's *The Psychiatrist and the Dying Patient*.[9] Freud discerns two primal urges, sexuality (*eros*) and aggression, which he sees as originally belonging together but later working independently. *Eros* serves the propagation of life, while aggression is linked with the desire, also a characteristic of life, to return to the primal state of death. Freud regarded this theory as metapsychological, a theoretical adjunct which he did not necessarily expect even his most faithful disciples to accept. He did not consider it essential for psycho-analysis. We have already seen that in the face of death man has ambivalent feelings. On the one hand it is frightening, *mysterium tremendum*; on the other, it is enticing, *mysterium fascinans* (the terms are taken from Rudolf Otto, *The Idea of the Holy*). It is by no means clear what it is in death that is *tremendum*, what *fascinans*, but we may perhaps say that the *fascinans* is the (psychic) experience of the death wish, the longing for the primal state of rest with the mother, while the *tremendum* is man's resistance against his aggression, against the threat of 'castration' by the father-figure.

(*d*) We do in fact observe this ambivalence of fear and desire towards death around us. The fear is obvious to us all, but the desire for death comes to the fore in times of depression, in people who are 'accident-prone' and have a sub-conscious desire which is revealed in their many mishaps, and maybe also in older people approaching the end of their days.

(*e*) Something which sheds a good deal of light on our modern situation is the way in which death is in a sense banished from the realities of normal life. The sick are taken to hospitals to die there; the dead are no longer left to lie at home but are removed to mourning parlours, and their earthly remains are 'touched up' to look pleasing, something which has become quite a vogue in the United States. Even before the war Heidegger made the contention that man seeks to ward off consciousness of death one of the cornerstones of his philosophy. We are entitled to state that, as with suffering, so there is a growing unwillingness to accept death. The farmer's wife who explained to me that she had decided not to let a cancerous growth be operated on, despite a favourable prognosis, because she had in her fifty-seven years found fulfilment in life, is an exception. In order to understand the climate of the modern hospital, it is necessary to recognize this growing unwillingness to accept death. The hospital of today with its newly-found therapeutic powers is the very place where the battle against death is most fiercely fought, often to the bitter end. It is part of the creed of the medical and nursing staff that death can never be accepted, and many patients find themselves caught up in this stand.

In ministering to the sick in hospital it is important to recognize that it makes a great deal of difference whether death is experienced as a possible, yet distant, eventuality or as a reality, close to and tangible. We need to consider both possibilities in more detail.

So long as death remains a possibility with which one has to reckon but which one need not take too seriously, one can attempt in some way to 'integrate' this experience into the whole pattern of one's life. Usually death is experienced as a threat which one seeks to ward off, possibly by forgetting about it, sometimes by a straight denial. The soldier on the battlefield counts on being spared; he believes, almost like a child, in his own immortality. Another, while in theory accepting the possibility, will in reality dismiss it. It is marginally possible to desire death or through fear of death to commit suicide. When Socrates defends himself in court in his *Apology*, death is as yet only a possibility; it can still be considered rationally and sensibly. Compared with the injustice done to him, death is the lesser evil; it is, moreover, but a dreamless sleep, or perhaps affords a chance to meet men of fame.

When, however, death draws tangibly near and we must

squarely face it, then a new element enters. We can see this in Socrates, among others. Now he speaks of the need to meet one's death in a positive way; he considers it ridiculous to fear death, now that it is closing in. The philosopher longs for liberation from the prison of his body: in the underworld he hopes, moreover, to discover the truth, pure knowledge. We may say, then, of Socrates that, while he does know fear, he nevertheless 'has' something in the face of death which is stronger than his fear, a certain longing. We find something similar, though within a wholly different framework of thought, when we turn to Paul. In II Cor. 5.6–9 he writes that he would rather be away from the body and be at home with the Lord. Whether Paul is at the time of writing facing the possibility of an imminent death is not clear, but we note that here also there is a longing which can take the apostle beyond fear. He can therefore meet death positively. Death is in a sense transcended, in that it brings about the realization of a new order for which man longs.

We could also argue that, in the face of approaching death, man is challenged to react, to become active. In the work already mentioned, Eissler seeks to throw light on the psychic factors which play a part in such reaction. He coins the word 'orthonasia', i.e. to guide and help an individual to find his personal way of meeting death and to help him to meet death freed from illusions, as opposed to euthanasia, i.e. to help someone through medical means to die without pain, if necessary by hastening the process of death. He contends that man through his sub-conscious desires resists death; the sub-conscious experiences death as a narcissistic humiliation and wants to continue living. I want to point out that he fails to draw attention to the fact that we may also in the sub-conscious find a desire for the peace of death. It seems to me that man's inner attitude towards death is ambivalent. Eissler wants to lead man to acceptance at the level of the intellect through a scientific approach: not to comfort but to help him recognize reality. He writes: 'Death becomes a natural event which can be integrated by reason, even if it cannot be integrated by the sub-conscious.'[10] In his view death, while physiologically the same for all men, can nevertheless become an individual and personal experience. Each man can, like Rilke, die his own death, in the same way that the sexual act, besides its common natural side, also has a highly personal aspect. Man, continues Eissler, is challenged by death. Each man must give his own answer to that challenge. This will have to include an acknowledgement of the objective significance of death. Without surrendering to illusions man must squarely face up to the truth, but the truth, however bitter it may prove to be, can enlarge a man's inner self which can thus attain a greater measure of freedom, despite the knowledge that the reality of which he is part is pitiless.[11]

This same conflict is movingly described by Simone de Beauvoir in *A Very Early Death*.[12] What we have here is in essence a heroic acquiescence in the inevitable. It is no accident that Eissler ends his dissertation by pointing us to the ancient Greek myth that man has sprung from the blood of the Titans. He observes that this myth may well come nearer to the psychological truth than that of the Old Testament, where man is created out of the dust. The Titans are those who seek to be God and thus to transcend the reality of death. We find this same thought in Sartre, who declares at one and the same time that God is dead and that we men must become gods. It should be clear that the accents placed by Eissler may lead – probably unintentionally – to the danger of stimulating narcissistic fantasies, thus tending to remove men from the reality of death rather than to help them to react to it in an objective manner. He himself shares with us his observation that his patients lived in a state of regression. What is, however, without doubt a concept of real importance is the idea that man is challenged by the approach of death and that he goes to meet this challenge in one way or another: his dying is not just a matter of fading away but rather an act, something he does, a personal reaction.

Karl Jaspers counts death to be one of those boundary situations which spell danger for man and are inscrutable. In the second volume of his *Philosophie*, which bears the title *Illumination of Existence*, he explains that these are the situations over which we have no control, to which we can only commit ourselves, as it were jumping into the deep. Other situations in our life we may be able to survey and even alter, but in such boundary situations, amongst which Jaspers places guilt, suffering and death, it is not so: all our activity here makes no essential difference. They are simply there and we have to accept them. This acceptance is one of the most difficult tasks with which we are faced in our existence. Especially in the face of such situations we often fall back into childish patterns of reaction. As these reactions are sometimes met with in ministering to the dying, I want to describe some of them.

In some people, more commonly in those condemned to death than those in hospital, the approach of death causes a complete disintegration marked by uncontrollable sobbing and screaming such as that of a child: the person is no longer himself. Another reaction is to ignore death completely. Amongst those condemned in the French revolution one often found a devil-may-care pose, while in hospital one finds the dying escaping and clinging to falsehood, unwilling to face the truth of the situation. A third reaction is the attempt to forget. Under the looming threat of German invasion in 1939 Warsaw was steeped in an atmosphere of festivity: people 'enjoyed' the beautiful summer weather. The man condemned to death relishes his last meal. Those who are sick sometimes enter a state of extraordinary euphoria.

There is a considerable advance towards maturity when we find people trying to come to terms with death in an agnostic and positive way. This is in essence the attitude advocated by Eissler. Despite its protest against the pitiless character of death, there is in this attitude an element of genuine confidence in the reality of human life. Eissler shows that the pre-condition for such a positive acceptance is something very much like the 'basic trust' which Erikson considers to be essential to a true wholeness of life. An important aspect is a man's relationship to his fellow men. One can accompany another in this meeting with death, journey with him for part of the way. There can be real comfort here, sometimes felt in a childish way, but at other times as a mature experience. We will return shortly to this aspect, which is of such vital importance. Another reaction may be that of blaming people. Such aggression is born from the fear of being deserted, left alone, and it is directed at those who are to stay behind, from whom one has not received sufficient support. Eissler has some shrewd observations on this aspect of a man's relationship to those who are to survive him.

Finally, there is the important reaction of the martyr. The martyr goes out to meet his death in the conviction that it will serve some good purpose, that it is not without meaning, or that it will open his eyes to the reality of another order of existence, which cannot be touched by death. Members of the resistance facing the firing squad would shout 'Long live our country!', 'Long live the Queen!', and Christian martyrs had visions of Christ, longing to 'be with the Lord'. One could say that this is the reaction characteristic of the *believing* person.

If we now try to draw some conclusions from all this material, we will find that there are basically three aspects of the experience of dying which we need to distinguish.

(*a*) First in this experience there is a *reaction* in the dying person, a reaction which may take very different forms, depending on personality, on whether death is imminent or not, on the awareness of support from others or of being alone, and finally on the presence of faith.

(*b*) The second aspect is that of *fear*. We have seen that this fear of death is probably linked with what Freud calls fear of castration. In people brought up in certain religious circles we find this fear of castration sometimes displaced by a fear of judgment, which should probably be explained as springing from a linking of the fear of the judgment of God (the Father) on all our life with this fear (see p. 52).

(*c*) The third aspect is the presence of a *desire for death*, which remains present both in and alongside the fear of death. We have pointed out an ambivalence in the face of death. There is a primal urge towards the peace of being hidden in the womb of our existence; death for many is the experience of returning to the reality from which we have sprung. In the patriarchal culture of ancient Judaism, dying was described as 'being gathered to one's fathers'. I suspect that the desire to be 'with the Lord' could be similarly understood. In our culture the predominant imagery is maternal, the earth, the womb, etc. Closely linked to this seems to me to be the dying man's sense of belonging to the family. The big question in a hospital is always whether the family should be told. We have the feeling that death and origin are closely linked: somehow the family, the womb from which we have sprung, must be present now. Eissler has rightly observed that to stay with the dying, to watch by him, is to accompany him, to die in some way with him. To experience precisely at this time our togetherness as a family, bound to one another in a common bond, to explore and experience the mystery of our origin together with the dying person, is in a sense to die with him, to accept, as it is sometimes put, that he has 'gone before' us.

Against the background of this general and introductory study of the experience of dying, particularly in the setting of a modern hospital, we can now look at pastoral ministry to the dying. What light is shed by all this on the minister's task? At this stage it is not our concern to define the task – we will be discussing the content of this ministry in full later – so much as to pinpoint and analyse the difficulties the minister is likely to encounter in carrying out his ministry in a modern hospital. For the time being we will define pastoral ministry to the dying as giving them the support needed to depart this life with genuine trust in God. What, then, are the problems that will arise in this respect?

It should be clear by now that dying in a modern hospital is a complicated emotional experience. Let us examine more closely some aspects which are of particular significance for the minister. The dominant climate in the modern hospital is that of the utmost resistance to death. In this climate the patient is the object of intensive medical care, often involving specialists from various disciplines. The thought that all this treatment has, considering the patient's condition, little chance of success is suppressed as far as possible. We find, rather, that both in the deliberations of the medical staff with one another and in their discussions with the patient, constant allowance is made for the possibility of success with new and different treatment. If finally death appears really inevitable, then the patient is immediately moved to a separate room, so that in the whole of the hospital there is no overt sign of the reality of death. One might well argue that the whole atmosphere of the hospital is geared to concealing the reality of death from the patient and his family. This really marks a radical change from the situation which obtained only some decades ago, when for many serious illnesses death was regarded as the 'natural' outcome, for which the patient and those close to him would inwardly prepare themselves. Another dominant feature of the modern hospital is the objective clinical approach to death. It is a physiological phenomenon, which the medical staff seek to prevent but at a certain stage have to accept as unavoidable.

Where the doctor has any religious belief, he will normally regard it as a personal matter which runs parallel to his medical work and often also to his dealings with patients. This sort of thing is the personal business of the dying, perhaps of the family and the clergy, but not of the doctor. There is therefore seldom any discussion of religious belief between doctor and patient. The nurse is in rather a different position. She will often find herself drawn into the discussion of religious issues by the patient and the family. In a sense she stands midway between the medical staff and the patient's personal circle. This creates a real problem for her, in that she has had no training in coping with this and therefore has difficulty in distinguishing the limits of her role. It seems to me that more attention to the problems of this situation in the training of the doctor would enable him to assess more effectively his role towards the patient who is beyond treatment, making allowance for differences about religious belief. On the whole his role at present would be defined as the provision of good medical care and rest, but what is meant by rest is left vague and is very much a matter of personal opinion.

There are many factors in a modern hospital which tend to make the patient weak and thus encourage regression towards infantile behaviour patterns. He is alone, removed from familiar surroundings, the object of all sorts of complicated and often painful treatment, dependent on all sorts of official people, who in many respects stand in an objective, almost impersonal relationship to him, and he is often prey to anxiety about the outcome of his illness. For this reason he is often seen to sway between an almost childish faith in the magical powers of modern medicine and a depressing fear that it will all be no good. We ought also to recognize that the very impressiveness of the modern technical equipment at the disposal of today's medical staff suggests to some patients that their condition must be serious, a notion they sometimes find it hard to resist.

When in a modern hospital the condition of a patient deteriorates to such an extent that death has to be reckoned with, certain steps are taken, which need to be mentioned, as they affect the pastor's ministry.

1. In order to alleviate pain and enable the patient to rest, he is often given special medicines which have an effect on the psyche, often making him sleepy and dull, occasionally inducing a state of euphoria, so that pastoral contact becomes more difficult and such conversation as one is able to have tends to assume an air of unreality.

2. After the long and exhausting struggle against the feared and inevitable end the patient, on realizing the seriousness of the situation, will sometimes react distinctively. Either he relapses into a state of deep and impenetrable despair or he experiences a sense of freedom at the knowledge that he will soon be released from his suffering. It is usually difficult to be of much use in either case.

3. The relationship with the family creates a difficult problem in the modern hospital. We have seen how deeply important the companionship of the family is to the dying. This is, of course, difficult to arrange in a hospital, where the patient is constantly being attended to by the medical and nursing staff, and where

there is little possibility of accommodating the family overnight to enable them to be at hand, should the situation become worse. The feeling of isolation which already hangs over the dying is made even deeper. Simone Beauvoir has given us a moving description of this in *A Very Early Death*. The sense of safety and security created by being together is much less easily given to those who die in hospital.

4. In Simenon's book *The Patient*, the nurse clearly plays a special part in the patient's emotions. I have found this insight confirmed in the diary of one who was seriously ill, which I was privileged to read. Simply by her presence, i.e. not only through her caring activity, the nurse can afford a measure of the sense of safety and security needed. She appears to represent the maternal aspect of existence (of our origin), which makes bearable the fear of non-being, of an-nihil-ation (castration) allied to it. Simenon describes how his patient feels the difference, is unhappier, when the nurse leaves the room. We have all had similar experiences, when we found mother out on coming home. Witness, too, the many tales of the child cut off from its parents and left to face the threat of terrifying Nothingness in the guise of giant or wolf, bent on devouring its prey. The presence of the nurse, then, has a definitely positive significance for the dying.

5. In the modern hospital, any relationship to a minister has an ambivalent character. He is a symbolic figure – spoken of as 'man of God' in the diary mentioned above – a symbolism often linked with dying. His mere presence can, for some fearful patient, uncertain about the outcome of his illness, confirm a suspicion that the end is near. Simenon describes this effect, and most clergy know that their arrival will be taken by some as a sign that they have been 'given up'. The reverse is also the case, that the minister stands in the patient's thoughts for some positive, meaningful perspective on death. This may be captured in the phrase 'man of God'. He represents the love of God, which is stronger than death. But the symbolic value of the clergy only remains significant and effective if the minister is prepared to draw near, to become, in Eissler's terms, a companion on the

way and one who will let himself be experienced as such. He can make God's love tangible through working through to a measure of solidarity with the dying, ready to listen to him, to share in his dying: it is then that the word of the gospel can become a liberating power. Experience shows that the gospel message has no effect when it is 'tossed to' the sick from a distance; it is effective only when it is born in the kind of relationship pictured above.

6. As the minister develops such a relationship with the dying person, he will also be drawn into a special relationship with the family. With them, too, he is making a journey. He shares in their vigil with the dying one. It follows that he also has a ministry to them. To them also he must be a listener; he must help them to be with the dying person in a useful way, to accept his going and later to cope with their mourning.

Finally, we may conclude that the pastoral ministry in the modern hospital is above all a matter of relationships. In the last analysis, what counts is not the minister's theological or psychological training but whether he has learnt to feel his way into the loneliness of the sick and the dying and whether he understands the emotional problems with which they are wrestling. He must, moreover, be able to sense in what way he is being used as a symbolic figure, as this will influence his approach. Naturally a sound academic training in theology and psychology is needed for such a ministry, but these will not suffice in themselves. He will need training of another kind.

When Rilke published his ideas about the need for a truly personal death, they caused considerable interest among clergy. He expressed them in his *Notebook of Malte Laurids Brigge*,[13] a writing which sprang from the conditions in which men died in the vast Parisian hospital, L'Hôtel de Dieu, which to him appeared like some grim death-producing factory. In a famous poem from his *Book of Hours*, he utters a prayer for each man to be given a death that matches his life and comes from it. To Rilke death is a humiliation, degrading and mean. To search for a personal death is thus to seek some circumstance which can at least give death a heroic dimension, some noble side, as, say, in death on the battlefield. It is to look for a proper dying. We have no business to delude ourselves about the grim reality of death, but must aspire in death to be Titanic, must assume a divine role. We may recognize in Rilke a wholly justifiable longing that we should die in a manner fit for human beings. Granted that death is a physiological, natural event, nevertheless it is also the death of a *person*, a personal affair. This means that every man hopes that his death will match his life, be in harmony with the identity discovered as a human being, worthy of that humanity, yes, and more, worthy of the ideals and beliefs by which he has lived. We hope that in our dying we will prove true to ourselves, true to the way we have sought to live.

Let us try to probe these ideas a little further. In the first place we hope for a humanly worthy death, i.e. that we shall not pass away like animals, unaware of what is happening. To be more specific: we hope to die in full awareness, having taken leave of those around us, leaving our affairs sorted out. The question must then be raised, whether this is really what everyone desires. Are there not many whose sudden and unexpected end, in which they were wholly unaware of events, should be described as 'a good way to go'? Doctors maintain time and again that the person who wants to know and can bear the knowledge is, in their experience, the exception. In the light of all that has been said above about people's reactions to distant and imminent death, it should be clear that in such statements there is an element of wisdom based on experience. It is quite true that many people would indeed take the news that they were incurable as a death-sentence. But is this still so later on? It is my impression that the situation changes with the approach of death. However that may be, we are not entitled to let human frailty compel us to abandon the ideal of a truly worthy human death.

Secondly, we hope for a death which will measure up to the ideals by which we have sought to live. We hope that we shall be able to meet our dying without excessive fear and certainly without forced behaviour or a display of exhibitionism or hysterics Again, we must ask whether all are able to cope in this way. We know how powerful our sub-conscious forces can be. It is the man who has learnt to live realistically who is best prepared to face death. In the light of our remarks about 'journeying with' and 'dying with' the dying it is understandable that the relationships with the family and with the hospital staff are important factors. Again, an emotional awareness of something which transcends death can help significantly in dying a worthy death. Examples of this are the martyr of the resistance and the convinced believer.

Finally, we hope for a death which will match our beliefs. For the believer, both death and life are holy mysteries which can only be understood in the context of the greater mystery of all that is. It holds good for our faith that both death and life find their final place in the Kingdom of God, that God, to use a human metaphor, rules over both and that in both we are bound to him. Belief in his judgment of our life and of the world may not be exclusively linked to our fear of death; it may only be one side of a positive relationship to God the Father.

We have now studied in some detail the two great issues which confront the minister in the modern hospital and the complex problems which cluster round them. More could be said about both, but we have been especially concerned to shed light on those aspects which mark out the particular task of the minister from those of others working in the hospital and thus to clarify his position in their midst. Against this background we now hope to be in a position to describe his role in the hospital.

# 5

# The Minister in the Hospital

In this chapter I shall attempt a more or less comprehensive sketch of the minister against the background we have seen in previous chapters. That in so doing we may recall ideas already dealt with is, in view of the task in hand, not altogether avoidable.

It seems to me that a discussion of the place of the minister in the hospital will only be worthwhile if we recognize as fundamental that in hospital one is dealing with a team, i.e. a group of people each with his own task and therefore with his own proper role, yet never allowed to forget that, for the sake of the patient, they must learn to play as a team. Hence it would be quite wrong to regard the minister as a figure on his own, one who has a task for which he is responsible only to himself and in which he must be allowed to go more or less his own way regardless of others. It follows that he simply may not see himself as someone who can pretend he is alone, who knows of course that he will have to fit his work in with that of doctors, nurses and others concerned with the patient, but needs only to make sure that he is not in the way too much.

One of the first concerns of anyone working in a hospital is to make the patient feel secure, i.e. to see that he does not begin to feel himself to be simply an object of multiple attention by all those who have such a variety of dealings with him, specialists, housemen, nurses, laboratory technicians, library and canteen workers, administrators, physiotherapists, family, and priests and ministers. It is of primary importance that patients should feel at home, important for their progress to recovery and because they have a right to be treated as fully human and not as objects to be manipulated at will. This being so, a first requirement is that those to whom they are entrusted should think and work together, so that patients will not have to cope with an atmosphere of division, jealousies and indifference, which would be guaranteed to fill them with fear and anxiety.

We all know that the hospital is a human institution in which the problem of relationships becomes steadily more acute as specialization and technical sophistication increase, management becomes more businesslike, and the actual work becomes more and more complicated. Hence we encounter the threat of failure to achieve a real measure of team-work and team-spirit despite good intentions and well-thought-out attempts to make these a reality. In the light of this one might be tempted to wonder whether there is any point in seeking to include the minister in a team which is already far from effective, even when coping purely with the patient's physical well-being. It might just be possible to succeed with a full-time hospital chaplain, but mostly we are dealing with visiting clergy or chaplains who come occasionally from surrounding districts and would therefore seem bound to remain foreigners in the hospital setting.

It is precisely this which makes me stress the team-principle. If we are to guard against turning the hospital into a factory in which only efficiency and production-figures are of importance, then we must grasp firmly that only a team of people, each an expert with his own task to do, yet able *as people together* to carry responsibility, can make a hospital into a community of human beings. If this does not happen at the top, it will certainly not happen lower down. I want to emphasize again, then, that it is fundamental that we seek to make the concept of team-work in hospital a reality. To explain *how* this is to be done is beyond the scope of this book, but I will attempt towards the end to work out how the minister might realistically find a place in such a team. The minister is therefore not an isolated person, who can be left to go his own way, but a man who in the midst of all the many ways in which the sick are cared for has his own way of caring, one which fits in with all the others, a man therefore who is in a real sense a colleague, a fellow-worker, primarily with doctor and nurse, but also with others such as the medical social worker.

This is not a simple matter, as the most junior trainee nurse will know. She senses the 'resistance' of the staff; the minister's visit can be inconvenient; he comes at an awkward moment; he simply enters, and, if he is not a regular visitor, he will be unknown; he often seems to do as he pleases and often appears on the ward against the wishes of other patients. She is in duty bound to let him carry on and is happy that he should do so, because she knows that patients sometimes need to talk over their problems with a clergyman, but could he not just have asked her whether it was all right? And could he not consult her, when so often she has information which could be helpful? Again, she will know the 'embarrassment' of which Barnes writes. It is difficult for us to see the minister as an ordinary person; there is an aura of mystery around him; he must somehow be 'other'. This makes it difficult just to go up to him. It is not easy for either the nursing or the medical staff to see in the minister a colleague and fellow-worker. This is because of the embarrassment and resistance pointed out by Barnes. Perhaps I am exaggerating the situation: this is better than to minimize the problem. We will only make improvements if we are prepared to take a cold, hard look at difficulties which may not always obtain but do occur frequently.

I am aware that the importance I have attached to the team-concept in the hospital needs to be argued more convincingly. As yet I have not defined the term. Earlier I have said that the concepts of *own role* and *playing together* are essential. But is that sufficient for a hospital? It may be so for a football team or group of travellers, though even there more is needed to produce team-work and team-spirit. A football team needs a captain, a travel-group a leader and guide. Moreover, the groups both need to be spared too much worry about practical matters. The threat of defeat for the one, prolonged foul weather for the other can become a gloomy burden. In the same way a great deal depends on the hospital management, its decisiveness and authority, in creating the chance of a sound team-spirit. The place needs to be efficiently organized so that members of the team are not hindered by poor lighting or lack of comfort or space. And one has to have a reasonably smooth run. Failure in operations, epidemics among patients are the kind of thing which adversely affect the team-spirit of the hospital. Taking the image further, we must say that it needs to be a *hospital-team*, a team like other teams yet with its own distinctive characteristics. Two of these need comment.

First, it is a therapeutic team, whose primary task is the cure of the patient. Secondly, it is a team with a central focus, the patient. It is his illness that calls the team into existence. Should there no longer be anyone to cure, the team would fold up. The hospital is therefore a task-centred group with a specific objective and, probably as a consequence, its own specific rules. In that we are dealing with a therapeutic team, there will be a hierarchy in the hospital. Everything serves the cure of the patient: hence the doctor stands at the head of the hierarchy. Everything in the hospital must be seen as subordinate to his insights, if need be, his orders. The modern hospital has seen the rapid development of an almost separate administrative and economic department, with which the medical staff have little to do, but in the last analysis these services, too, must be subordinate to the overriding general purpose of the hospital, the process of curing the sick.

This point of view is obviously significant for the pastoral ministry. The minister has his own task, with which the medical staff have little to do, but he is exercising this task in the domain of the doctor and stands within the hierarchy of which the latter is the head. Even if his work is not directly aimed at the recovery of the patient, which is the specific task of the doctor, nevertheless it is aimed at the total well-being of the patient, in which the doctor also declares an interest. The minister seeks to perform his task within the network of tasks performed in the process of curing the patient by doctors, nurses, and others, and, though virtually a guest, with the aid of the staff will often have to sort out his place within this network. This will not be quite so difficult for the full-time chaplain or the rector of a church hospital. He knows the situation and will gradually work out his place within it. Ministers and priests coming in from outside find the adjustment much more difficult. I believe that the 'resistance' of the hospital staff mentioned above has something to do with this. In a book written for nurses as well as clergy it is perhaps worth pointing out that clergy coming in often feel very unsure of themselves. A great deal of apparently 'clumsy' behaviour probably results from this. The minister is uncertain, because as a healthy person he suddenly comes into a place where he imagines suffering and dying behind every closed door and suspects the theatre, which he has never been in, to be a kind of modern 'torture chamber'! His uncertainty is increased by the unfamiliar labyrinth of rooms and corridors, in which he gets lost, and the host of men and women in white, of whose status and function he has little idea and amongst whom he feels a stranger. There is the tale of the clergyman who on occasional visits to the hospital carefully walked at a respectful distance round the white clad figure of the barber! How was he to know it was not the specialist? Clearly the nursing staff in particular can do a great deal to put the clergy at ease.

I should add at this point that there is a gap in the training of clergy in this field. It would be good if they could work in a hospital for a spell. It would enable them to realize how best to be a 'guest' in the hospital, to ask for the ward sister and consult her, to understand that the primary concern of the hospital must be the physical care of the patient and that in some cases one should discuss with the sister or the doctor whether pastoral help would be an aid and when to see the patient.

We have emphasized that the hierarchy with the medical man at its top is a characteristic of the hospital team. We need to examine this structure a little more closely, as it is especially in the nature of this hierarchy that a number of changes are evident, which affect the minister's position. In former times, this hierarchy was distinctively paternal. The old-fashioned hospital was a sort of family, with a father, the director of the hospital, stern mothers, the matrons, and for younger or older children the trainee and qualified nurses, who were seldom considered adult. Father and mother took care of everything, and their authority was unquestioned. Hospital life was communal like that of the old-fashioned ship, and was marked by strict rules and clearly defined authority-structures.

This paternalistic pattern is rapidly disappearing in the modern hospital, though traces of it still remain, as witness Gerda Cohen's *What's Wrong with Hospitals?* The paternalistic hierarchy is being replaced by one which could be described as *functional*. This means that the team is increasingly a community of people *working* together, in which there is a much greater sense of equality and freedom in personal relationships. Some of the obvious signs of this change are that nurses are increasingly living out of the hospital, that the patterns of authority are altering and individuals are considered to be capable adults.

These changes, which can be observed throughout modern society, naturally create all sorts of new problems. Personal contact decreases, more depends on individual responsibility, many things have become more uncertain than they were, and personal relationships have, in the hospital as elsewhere, become full of problems. This is not the place to pursue this issue, except to point out that the situation affects the position of the minister. In the older hospital he could normally, with the aid of the director or one or two of the senior sisters, manage to find a place for himself and be accepted: the hospital was usually small and it would not be long before everyone knew him and made room for him. This is no longer true. Like the specialist, the registrar, the analyst and others, the minister is a figure with his own role to play, and if he wishes to be accepted, he will have to make that role very clear. He will have to stake his claim, or rather a claim for his kind of caring for the patient, and work out with those in charge of the ward how best his work fits in. He has become only one in a long queue of workers for whom the ward sister has to find a place: the registrar, the social worker, the analyst, the physiotherapist, those concerned with rehabilitation and the care of souls.

The functional character of the team is much more pronounced. There is much less personal contact, and consultation is on a functional basis. This causes considerable difficulty for the minister, especially if he has learned the early lessons of his ministry in the relatively simple relationships of a village community and has developed his approach to people in that setting. Sometimes he will attempt to overcome his problem with a naively jovial approach, only to find that this cuts no ice in the modern hospital. Here also there could well be an improvement in clergy training. Of course he will learn to find his way, if he comes to work in the city or has often to visit hospitals, but the so-called 'embarrassment' of the hospital staff towards clergy would be rather less if they met fewer clergy whose behaviour in a modern environment was so clumsy and naive.

There is a point of view through which many of the problems engendered by the functional character of the hospital team could be solved to a considerable extent. It lies in the conscious realization that the team has a focus for which it exists, which has called it into being, namely the patient. All the problems that can trouble human relationships, prestige, jealousy, rancour and fear, could vanish in the realization that it is the patient for whose sake all are called to work together. The patient brings us together, determines our relationship to one another, helps us in the team to listen and pay attention to each other. I believe that the minister likewise will always find his place in the team, so long as he lets this place be determined by the needs of the patient, by his contribution to the patient's well-being, and always seeks to establish, where necessary with others involved, where his care for the sick fits in best with the care of others. In this way the minister could learn to discover his place in the team, and one hopes that doctors and nurses would, for their part, help to fulfil it.

There is another aspect which we cannot afford to ignore. If they are to work properly functional relationships require a good understanding between those concerned. In the older paternalistic set-up this was not quite so important, as the structure authority was so unmistakable that orders would be carried out irrespective of good or bad understanding. There might be moans; one might feel unappreciated or slighted, but the work was done. Functional relationships need to be oiled to run smoothly. People involved must be able to get on with each other. This does not mean that they need to become close friends or even to see very much of each other out of working hours, but it does mean that they need to be reasonably sympathetic to each other and to enjoy working together. In the hospital, as in the factory or the office, people must be able to get on well with each other. Work on the ward runs more smoothly where the relationships between members of the nursing staff and between nurses and medical men are good.

This is obviously also true of the minister's work. While the regular hospital chaplain or rector soon realizes this, visiting clergy are, in my experience, less aware of this. The minister must never forget that he will find his task much easier where he is on friendly terms with the staff. We all know from experience that good work-relationships are so often blocked by our habit of stereotyping others with whom we have to do, without knowing them at all well. Many clergy are lumbered with the notion that the nurse is a terribly busy person who will find it irritating to have him in the way. Nurses often find visiting clergy whom they don't know well 'silly' or 'weird', or they fear they might upset patients with their notions. Such stereotypes do have their roots in experience. When we have come across some clergy or nurses like that, we are tempted to think that they are all the same. But stereotypes also have roots in our own sense of uncertainty. Clergy think of themselves as a nuisance and hence expect the nurses to find them so. The nurse feels a little unsure of herself in the presence of the clergy and soon reacts negatively. And yet the clergy and nurses we tend to cast in such moulds are usually very normal people, who in fact would be pleased to be of help. I consider it important that we, staff and clergy, should more consciously create opportunities of meeting and getting to know and appreciate each other: I want to come back to this point at the close of this chapter.

Up to this point we have taken some soundings in the atmosphere of the modern hospital and have pointed out some of the opportunities and difficulties of the minister's position in the team which works there. The time has now come to give a more concrete description of what the minister might talk about and what he does. This will be the subject of the next section.[1]

As nurses we see the minister at work. He talks with the patient. If he is a Protestant, he may read to him from the bible or pray with him. If he is a Roman Catholic priest, he may hear confession; he may distribute communion (often after mass in the morning in the chapel); where the patient is seriously ill, he may bring it to him in bed. What does all this mean?

Let us assume that the reader of this book has no idea of the task of a minister or priest and try to explain what the contact of both of them with the patient involves. We begin with a look at the minister. If he is a visiting minister, he will be the minister of the congregation to which the patient belongs. Where he is a regular hospital chaplain, the situation is a little different. He is in that case the appointed representative of the church to which the patient belongs, standing in for their own minister. In the last few years denominational differences have become less significant: hence the chaplain in the hospital will to a considerable extent represent the 'Church' (with a capital letter), of which the denominations are different forms. There is still a noticeable difference between the Roman Catholic and the Protestant churches, but here, too, there is by now an increasingly intimate co-operation between their 'officials'. What, then, does the minister do?

We observe how he goes to the patient's bedside and greets him, and we hear him ask how the patient is getting on, how the operation went. Gradually a conversation develops in which we see the minister listen a great deal and occasionally, with a serious face, make some remark. The conversation may end in several ways: some ministers will draw a bible from their pockets and read a passage and then pray with the patient: some clergy like to leave a booklet or leaflet behind them: sometimes the conversation closes with a simple handshake.

Visiting the sick has at all times been part of the pastoral ministry. It is specifically named beside the tasks of leading worship, religious instruction, visiting members of the congregation, when the pastoral ministry is defined. One has to remember that in Christendom the sick have long been the object of special care. With the poor, the widows and orphans, they belonged to those who stood outside the community, who could not fend for themselves and often faced wretched hardship. It was one of the works of Christian compassion to provide shelter for them and to visit them. The hospital was originally more such a place of refuge and shelter for the sick than a place for cure and recovery. The minister would visit the sick as part of his commission, the task to 'comfort the sick', to comfort them by proclaiming and expounding the good news as given in the bible, the news that Christ lived among men as the sign of God's love for us and wants to bring all men to faith in God through his church, to belief in a new and everlasting life. To comfort someone really means to open up for him a new and liberating perspective in a difficult situation. It was the task of the minister to give to the sick, who were often literally 'without hope', the perspective of this new and other life, in this way to prepare them, if need be, for death, and at all times to strengthen their faith. There used even to be fixed formulae for such conversations.

So much has changed in the last few decades in the hospital, in the care and treament of the sick, and in our attitude towards illness and being ill, that we could well speak of a revolution. It is a change which has also affected the pastoral ministry to the sick. This ministry is still one of the special tasks of the clergy, but it is no longer understood as the kind of comfort described above, which was so very much linked with the circumstances of another age. Of course, even today, there are still areas where people think within old patterns: we still meet clergy visiting in hospital with this purpose, but on the whole the pastoral approach to the sick is now changing under the impact of change in the hospitals themselves. We can see a similar change taking place in the Roman Catholic church, where Extreme Unction, the last sacrament of the dying, is changing in accent (see above). Essentially the structure has remained. The minister comes as the representative of the church; he comes to help; he seeks to give support to overcome sickness in faith; and for this he needs the well-tried aids of bible-reading and prayer. Nevertheless, there has been a radical change in the shape and the setting of his conversation with the sick.

The minister is no longer the impressive, awe-inspiring father-figure of former times, nor the comforting fatherly 'shepherd' who plays down his role; rather, he seeks to be one who immerses himself in the situation of the sick, who sheds light on their difficulties, who helps them to find a new way through the uncertainty which is so characteristic of present-day belief. A 'shepherd', but in a new style; not one who considers the 'sheep' immature and deals with them by paternalistic suggestion, but one who in the burden and heat of the day walks with them for a while, above all one who as shepherd stays 'with' them and discloses the presence of that great Shepherd, the Christ, whom, in the full meaning of the word, he re-presents. He seeks to be the hand of Christ reaching out through his church to his followers. He is above all simply a man, a fellow human being, who has his own problems, so very much the same as those faced by the sick. He understands the problem of suffering, the absurdity, the difficulty of illness and death in a society which is technically so highly advanced, the empty meaninglessness of road accidents, of incurable disease, of unbearable pain. He, too, walks the hard road and searches with the sick up blind alleys for light on the way, such as can suddenly break out from a word of Christ or about Christ in the bible. The light cannot simply be switched on on demand, for the minister is a man with all his uncertainties, but he can, to use an expressive current image, be a beggar who can tell another beggar where perhaps he may find bread. In this spirit he will listen to those things the sick want to share with him, and seek with them, in the inscrutable situation they uniquely experience, for that which may prove to be 'bread'. The bible here is not a source-book of solutions and answers, but a log-book in which those who have journeyed close to Christ have recorded light found on the way, so that we too might be helped on our way.

The work of a Roman Catholic priest is different in form, though it is essentially about the same things. For the nurse in particular, however, it is important to be aware of the differences. I am basing my description on observations by Dr W. J. Berger, a Roman Catholic priest attached to the Catholic University of Nijmegen as lecturer in pastoral psychology. One difference which immediately catches the eye is that the work of the Roman Catholic priest is marked less by words than by actions. The minister is called a servant of the word of God (*verbi divini minister*), while the most characteristic task of the priest is the administration of the sacraments. Of course, the priest also talks with the sick – a great deal more emphasis is now placed on this – and of course the minister is entitled not only to proclaim the word but to administer the sacraments of baptism and the last supper (the two sacraments, sacred acts, which Protestant and Roman Catholic have in common). But the emphasis is different, more on the word with one, on the sacrament with the other. It may make the relationship clearer when we see that the sacrament makes visible the word which the minister proclaims and the sick seek to believe.

We can say, then, that both minister and priest are, despite differences, essentially at one, in that both word and sacrament point to the one to whom the patient tries to entrust himself. For example, the washing away of sin in which the baptized believes. The lighting of a candle makes visible the burning up of life. The feeding with bread in the eucharist is or means the strengthening of life. Anointing with oil is a symbol of support for the sick and the bread of the eucharist provision for the last journey. When, in the name of Christ, the priest gives absolution, he makes the sign of the cross over the sick, symbol of the cross of Christ which is the source of all forgiveness.

There has lately been an increasing desire to discuss the meaning of these signs. Both patient and priest want to experience them in a fitting manner. The priest will seek to help the patient to understand how he sees his life, what faith means for him, what significance it brings to his life and how that significance may grow deeper. One could perhaps say that the priest as much as the minister tries to accompany the patient to the point where the sacrament can convey its saving power most fully and bring the sick in touch with Christ.

Those who work in hospital will know how often a sense of peace can come to the sick through the priest's visit and the giving of the sacrament. The act can bring this peace more easily than the word, which has to be understood and digested, and which, when not clearly understood, can make a patient fret. The action of the priest makes clear and beneficial what a man through his illness cannot at this moment grasp. People can draw nearer to each other through deeds and gestures than through words. There is, moreover, the truth that our human words can never contain the ineffable, the holy mystery, which lies at the heart of faith. The actions of the priest point to Christ, his words and deeds, which for those who believe in them reveal the way to God. In his way the priest, through his actions, also makes Christ, the 'Shepherd', who wants to lead men to God, present. He is Christ's re-present-ative.

The place of the Roman Catholic priest in the life of the hospital is therefore not really very different from that of the Protestant minister. In the past the 'rector' of a small, old-fashioned church hospital might well have sought to turn the place into a church, e.g. by distributing the sacrament to the sick after mass in the chapel in a sort of solemn procession. The modern hospital is, as far as the Roman Catholic is concerned, primarily a hospital.

As we shall see later, the presence of the priest in the hospital, like that of the Protestant minister, helps to save the place from becoming a 'cure-factory': it becomes a place in which people can pass through the crisis-situations of suffering and dying in a human way and can be helped to do so in faith. Their presence is a sign that the hospital seeks to give every man the freedom to live or die in a personal way. In this freedom the minister has an important part to play. It is his task to accompany men to a true living and a true dying, life and death experienced in the light of God. This does not make him a 'heavenly sales-man'; it does not mean that he has to 'be ready with' the sacra-ment when there is danger of death. It is for him to stand by the sick and be with him in this crucial journey, and also to help his family to stand by him in the same way. Suffering and death, which for the hospital staff spell defeat and hence must be kept out of view, are a challenge for both the priest and the Protestant minister, an opportunity through their support to help a life to come to its fulfilment, its true end, as Christ cried on the cross 'Finished!'

We have now given a fairly full description of the work of the minister, whether he be Protestant or Roman Catholic, and yet this picture of his work is incomplete. If we are to give a true account of what it is we do and what we have to say as ministers in the hospital, then we must look at the minister's contribution and sketch his relationship to the other members of the staff in greater depth. I intend to do this through the somewhat unusual comparison of the minister in hospital with the clown in a circus. I trust that it will become quite clear that this comparison is not a trivial one, but has a deep significance.

I would argue that the clown is a necessity in the circus, without whom the circus is no longer a circus but is reduced to a string of numbers, and that the clown occupies a unique place among the other artists in the circus. There are three tensions in the life of the clown: first, the tension between being a member of a team and being in isolation: secondly, the tension of appearing to be and feeling like an amateur among acknowledged experts: and finally, the tension between the need for study and training on the one hand and the necessity to be original and creative on the other. It should not prove difficult to make the connection with the minister's position.

In his striking novel *The Clown*,[2] the German author Heinrich Böll has drawn a moving picture of the clown. The book describes the thoughts and feelings of a professional clown who has been deserted by the woman who has shared his life for some years and with whom he has been deeply in love. She has left to marry a man who is a social 'success', a leading member of his church. In his reaction to this the clown makes clear to us what the essential character of clowning is about. The clown is one who cannot feel at home among those who are so successful: they make him feel powerless, weak: in the standards and clichés of normal life he senses the superficial and the spurious. He lives, as it were, on a different wavelength; he is one who, despite all his outward clumsiness and failure, nevertheless comes across to us as a man who comes close to what life is really about. He knows the meaning of love, of sorrow, of solidarity. These are things that those who make a fortune or a name for themselves, who sit in the front row, never find. The clown makes us feel nostalgic. We find him pathetic and laughable, but he represents something in ourselves; we somehow see in him something of what we ought really to be like. Charlie Chaplin and Buziau spoke to thousands because they managed to show the ability to find the genuine, the authentic on the edges of life: the wry smile in the face of failure; the strange victory of the man who recognizes his weakness, his powerlessness in failure, and accepts it as part of the scheme of things; the little man who continues to have faith in something indestructible. Why *did* people flock to see the films of Chaplin and the revues featuring Buziau? Is it not because in the midst of this overpowering world with its armies and wars, its churches and politics, business empires and industries, and its vast cities, man still knows in his heart that he is only small, and he wants to recognize his small and powerless self in those little, funny people who play this part with a smile, who, playing like children amongst big guns, suddenly allow what is threatening to be seen for what it is, powerless and ridiculous. In this case the clown has a clear function. He puts things in perspective. He shows that there are more sides to life than those grasped by the big battalions. It is no accident that in the courts of the mighty the jester alone had the freedom to say what he liked. The jester reduced the ruler, who might have absolute power over life and death, to the stature of a man like others, and so made life bearable for the courtiers and, one suspects, for the ruler himself. Jesters fulfilled, in modern parlance, a psycho-hygienic function. This is also the function of the clown in the circus itself; that is why he belongs to it, this place in which people perform great feats, tame wild animals and do hair-raising stunts on the trapeze. They make us feel tense and frightened, but the clown puts it back in perspective. In a childish way he makes these stunt-men look a little foolish: he makes us feel that they are, after all, only human and ordinary, and thus re-establishes a sort of spiritual balance.

We have seen, then, that the clown has his own place in our world. He is much more than a joker, a funny guy. He brings home to us an aspect of life which we need to make the world tolerable. He has his own wavelength, his own pattern.

One of the remarkable phenomena of our time is the change which has overtaken the image of the priest and minister. They used to be regarded as the pillars of an ordered society, the upholders of morality, guardians of respectability, people of social standing, men of unmistakable authority. These features are gradually fading and giving way to a newly emerging shape, which bears a remarkable resemblance to the figure of the clown. How clearly this is captured in the Chaplinesque character of Don Camillo, known through books and films all over the world. Already in a previous century the famous Danish theologian, Kierkegaard, made use of this imagery in a now famous passage. We find clownish features in the novels of Bernanos and Graham

Greene (e.g. the whisky-soaked priest in *The Power and the Glory*). Many will be familiar with the figure of the idiot in Dostoievsky's novel of the same name. We are beginning to get a feel for 'the foolishness of God' in our world. How this can work out in reality is shown, for example, by the non-violent protest movement against racial segregation in the United States. To fight without resort to violence shows a touch of the clown. There are words in the New Testament which point to the reality of this 'foolishness of God'. In the first letter to the Corinthians, Paul speaks of the divine foolishness of the cross of Christ, who has allowed himself to be crucified: 'the foolishness of God is wiser than men, and the weakness of God is stronger than men'. And a little later, he observes that the Christian community does not consist of many influential or important people: 'God chose what is foolish in the world to shame the wise.' Christians are, therefore, according to Paul, called to be 'fools for Christ's sake'. Did Christ himself perhaps hint at this when he spoke of the need to be converted and become like little children? We are undoubtedly touching here on a real aspect of the New Testament understanding of faith.

It is not so easy to capture this aspect definitively in words. We can indicate it as follows: a character which is slightly anti-social; openness and sympathy in love; a feel for the fringes of human life; a kind of irresponsibility, carelessness and inner freedom; the ability to share suffering, compassion; humour (but normally not satirical humour!); a great deal of patience and wisdom. And we are to note that these are not experienced as normal human qualities but as a pattern of life of another order, on another wavelength. This is the life of a 'saint', in its deepest sense.

We noted earlier a threefold tension in the life of the clown, and also remarked that there was clearly a parallel here with the tensions of the minister in hospital. We must now look at the latter. First, there is the tension between belonging to a team and a measure of isolation. The clown is a member of a team: they value one another and have a certain sense of solidarity;

they respect each other's skills. At the same time, the clown has his own place, his 'number'; he is different from the others. Essentially he stands alone in the circus. In his work, he has little contact with the others. He represents a personal 'dimension'.

Clergy also find that it seems difficult for the medical staff to grasp the nature of their work, even when they make a real effort to do so. This is in the deepest sense the source of the lack of clarity noted by Elizabeth Barnes.

For the clown, the public is much more than an object of his prowess, as it is for the other circus artistes. He has a kind of solidarity with the public in the boundary situations of our existence: sorrow, the absurd, setbacks. Chaplin and Buziau have a relationship with the public which is peculiar to them. The clown tries to get the audience 'with him' in smiling in the midst of tragedy: he shows his littleness, but in so doing points to real greatness. In the same sort of way the minister in hospital is other than the medical men, for whom the patients become objects of their medical skills, to be 'treated'. Of course there is an element of solidarity with the patient, but the role of the doctor towards the patient demands objectivity. Here lies a real difference in the role of the minister. His solidarity with the patient is peculiarly his own, different from that of the doctor; it springs from a familiarity with the boundary situation. The solidarity of the doctor and patient is that of comrades-in-arms; that of the minister is that of standing with the patient in the difficulties and opportunities of boundary situations. In this solidarity the minister, like the clown, will seek to make himself small, but in so doing he will point towards the great things, which can set the sick man free, show him the (divine) humour of the situation, so that in the midst of his suffering he will raise a smile.

Like the clown, the minister also represents a different order, a separate wavelength, the world of faith, i.e. that of the man who discovers God at the centre of his life. Perhaps we may say that the world of the clown is that of the one who in the ultimate decaying of life asserts himself as truly human. It may well be that the two worlds are much closer to each other than one suspects.

The second tension experienced by the clown is between the awareness that he is amongst 'experts' and the fact that by comparison he is an 'amateur'. They do their stunts; he seems to contribute no such feats. In the hospital the minister experiences a similar contrast. Increasingly, the hospital is the scene of tremendous feats: between these walls great strides are made in the march of science and technology. Those working there are all experts in their own fields who have had a special training for their task. The specialists, nurses, social workers, analysts, physiotherapists – they are all trapese-artistes, but the poor clergyman is the clown. He presents a clear contrast to all of them. Paul, in the same letter to the Corinthians from which we quoted above, writes that his work among them in Corinth was not marked 'by plausible words of wisdom'. He does not trust that kind of stunt: he wants the work to be God's, and for that reason he must avoid putting himself in the limelight through cleverness.

The minister has a different sort of contact with the patient from that of other members of the team. He does not wear a white coat, is not conspicuous. In hospital he is just an 'ordinary' person. He may not rely on his learning or training, on a sympathetic personality, on a straightforward easy manner, nor on his seriousness, or the warmth of his approach, or his good reputation or even on his modesty. All these things can at any time get in the way of that which needs to come into being between him and the patient. The minister is only true to his calling when he does not draw attention to himself in any way whatever, but by his actions and his words points away to the one in whose service he stands, whom he represents and seeks to make present to the man in his sickness. There must be an *innocence* about him, though not gullible ignorance; he must be the one who knows the powers of darkness and temptation – indeed, no aspect of life should be foreign to him – yet also knows he can see and point to a way which surmounts them. He must therefore be naive, in the sense in which Christ spoke of becoming a child, an attitude constantly aware of its own opposite, fully understanding it. The minister who is just naive will not be able to understand and accept the other as he needs to be understood, as someone who has run to a stand-still in the blind alleys of existence. Paul could write about the value of 'foolishness', because his Jewish upbringing had instilled the experience of 'wisdom' and its lure into every fibre of his being.

The third tension is that between the necessity of study and training on the one hand and of originality and creativity on the other. If the minister is to be compared with the clown, he is not to overlook how Grock, one of the greatest of clowns, would study his act almost daily, frequently giving it fresh slants, and taking care to note the reactions of the audience. He realized that a clown had to be professional. The pastoral ministry is also a trade one has to learn and make one's own by study and training. It is encouraging to find that an increasing number of ministers in the Netherlands are now preparing for their ministry by taking part in a 'clinical training' course. Neither clown nor minister are innocents; they know what they are doing. Yet clergy will have to realize that too often their knowledge is not enough. They have too little insight into the patient and the way in which he has to wrestle with the problems of being ill; they realize too little that the business of creating a relationship with the sick is deliberate and a matter of continuous self-examination; more generally, they are too little aware of the fact that in purely professional terms they fall short of the mark in certain respects.

And yet, at the same time, the pastoral ministry can never be a question of routine and familiar ruts; at least it ought not to be. The minister, like the clown, must in the depths of his being remain original and creative. What does that mean in practice? For me it means that the minister also experiences the pangs of doubt and unbelief which the patient faces on his sickbed. It is when the minister thinks that his belief is a possession, to be handed out at will, that his ministry becomes a routine. He will only be able to listen to the doubt and the hidden unbelief in others (and without that he simply cannot be of help!) if he is also tuned to listen to the doubt and unbelief in himself.

It follows from this that he will need a community – preferably in the setting of his work, i.e. of colleagues – in which he can discuss the personal aspects of his work with others. Such exchange will shed light on points where he will not be able to provide such light himself, and where study and self-imposed meditation are also not likely to do so. Indeed, true study and real meditation are more likely to spring from such conversations. The isolation of the minister is on the one hand a condition of his ministry, but it can also endanger the reality of his work.

The reader will have noticed that my aim in this section is to create a measure of understanding of the minister and his task among the other members of the team by sketching the lines of the pastoral ministry as it were from within, to show how being a minister is experienced inwardly. In other words, we are not just looking at the task of the minister but also at the minister himself. The picture will therefore not be complete unless we go further and attempt to depict how the minister experiences this threefold tension and copes or fails to cope with it. I want to draw attention to three points, which need to be grasped by those who have dealings with the minister, if they are to have a clear understanding of him.

First, many clergy who come to work in institutions such as hospitals or prisons will, initially at any rate, suffer under a sense of inferiority. The others in the team seem to be so much better at their job; they can point to results; they are often more efficient. The minister is then exposed to the temptation to imitate the others and in some way or other to conform. He also tries to conduct his conversations after the manner of the psychiatrist or the social worker. He does not realize that in so doing he is, in missionary terms, 'going native'. He ceases to be himself. If he does not try this, he may fall into an opposite trap, in that he attempts to mark off his position in too self-assertive a fashion. He compensates for his unsureness through a show of authority; he makes it clear that he has rights and can expect co-operation.

Alternatively he quickly feels himself slighted and complains far more than is reasonable. It is simply a necessary aspect of working in a team that one has to learn to fit in with the work of others and that this involves a certain amount of 'give': nurses and medical staff have to learn a similar lesson. I am not sure how frequently such compensation occurs. Probably there is a great deal less of it than I might seem to suggest. What I am concerned to stress is that the position of the minister in the hospital not only creates uncertainty for the hospital staff but also for him. He is not always capable of judging his place, status and role clearly amongst the various experts in the hospital. The older man will probably have less difficulty, but the younger clergy especially will often not find their way around hospital life without problems.

The second point we must note is that in coping with the tensions indicated, the minister is also affected by the vast shifts which occur throughout our modern culture, creating difficulties in assessing his actual task and opportunities. Not only in the hospital but everywhere in modern society we meet a growing re-thinking of 'the place and task of the clergy in a new world'.[3] Some ministers sense this shift as an erosion of the pastoral ministry: the role, task and structure of the ministry seem to become diffused. The church and consequently the ministry suffer a loss of function in comparison with an earlier age; they are being penned into a small and clearly marked off area. More and more other social agencies are taking over work which used to be part of the church's task. There is a consequent and inevitable loss of authority. For example, when the Pope makes pronouncement in the field of modern scientific developments, these carry much less weight than they would have done in the last century. For some clergy this can result in a loss of belief in their contribution. We pointed this out in another connection. Everywhere in the church one finds the same discussion: What is the essence of the pastoral ministry? What is irreplaceable about it? And what, in the light of this, are the possibilities open to us of realizing this essential ministry?

It is clear enough that the work of the minister is different from that of the psychiatrist and the medical social worker. Of course there are points of contact, but it possesses something peculiarly its own, its own focal point. I believe that we will best grasp this if we say simply that the minister is the representative of the church. More is involved in this than the words might suggest, and it is here more than anywhere that we come on the track of the true character of the pastoral ministry. As a representative of the church the minister in fact seeks to represent Christ. It is true, of course, that every person may in his dealings with others and therefore with the sick know himself to be a follower of Christ. One can see one's work as nurse or doctor as service to Christ. Indeed, in a famous poem, Guillaume van der Graft says of the surgeon that, even if he himself does not believe in Christ, in the poet's eyes he still brings relief from pain for the sake of Christ. The minister, however, has been explicitly appointed by his church to represent Christ. At the Second Vatican Council, the Roman Catholic Church produced some new definitions of the church which appeal to me. The church is there described as the people of God, which in its earthly pilgrimage is being led by Christ into a future in the light. If to represent Christ means to make him present, then the consequence for the ministry is that the minister so stands by the other (i.e. more is involved than proclaiming the message or distributing the sacraments) that the other comes to accept that he belongs, that in the solidarity offered him by the minister he finds the courage to entrust himself to Christ and to the light. The pastoral ministry is therefore pastoral solidarity with the other, supporting him in the quest to become one who dares to believe in himself, because he has discovered through the minister, *experienced* through him, that Christ believes in him. As a result, he begins to look for that light in hope and in turn finds himself wanting and able to be in solidarity with others.

To represent Christ is therefore essentially a way of being (i.e. an interaction of word and deed), in the deepest sense an attitude. When we grasp this, we can see that the presence of the minister changes the 'climate' of the hospital: instead of being an institution it becomes a home. It becomes much more than a factory, a place in which 'feats' are performed. This happens in the same way in which the 'climate' of the circus changes through the presence of the clown, who by his performance puts the 'feats' of the others in perspective.

In a discussion about the significance of the pastoral ministry in the hospital a surgeon remarked that we need the minister for the climate, the spirit of the hospital. It is not that we want to have a certain reputation, that with us, as in church hospitals, there are services and that we therefore meet the wishes of those patients who value them: it is, rather, that we recognize that our medical work comes to stand in a different framework when the minister works beside us, a framework which we sense to be right. The hospital must be more than a factory. We could perhaps say that, just as the clown makes the circus what it truly is, so the presence of the minister makes the hospital truly itself. Through his place in it he sets the experts in a different perspective. He represents another wavelength, another order, in which man is no longer only an object of treatment, but a person, who struggles in his suffering to remain man, perhaps man with a relationship to God.

There is a third point. The minister can attempt to resolve the tensions inherent in his position by excessive activity. He thinks that he can justify his place in the hospital by *much doing*. The hospital is increasingly becoming a place in which people are busy with the patient. In earlier days, one of the features of the process of recovery was the rest which the hospital afforded the patient. The modern hospital, by contrast, is a beehive humming with endless activity. One of the prime considerations has become the need to shorten the average stay of the patient. This can only be achieved through being constantly and efficiently busy with the patient. It is tempting for the minister to try to compensate for his lack of certainty by also being busy with all sorts of things, lots of conversations, lectures, study groups, services, leaflets, in short, by being able to produce a long and impressive work list. Sometimes he feels he needs to justify his existence in this way.

Of course a minister needs to map out his work efficiently and to make good use of his time. Yet he must never forget that, in his ministry, what he is is more important than what he does. Decisive for the 'success' of his ministry is his ability to recognize that pastoral relationship in which he stands and on that basis to seek to create proper and good relationships. What matters is his attitude, whether he has a real interest in (which means 'being among') the patients, the staff, in all concerned, in the institution itself and – never forget! – in himself.

We have now considered the place of the minister in the hospital team and raised some of the problems he faces in being a minister in the complex situation of the modern hospital. I want to finish this chapter with some practical observations. Recently a memorandum was published in the military hospital, the Dr A. Mathijsen Hospital, in Utrecht, about 'the integration of spiritual care in the hospital'. The aim of this integration is to make those dealing with the spiritual welfare of the patients real members of the team. What must we do and what must we watch, if we want to prevent their effective isolation from the rest of the team? The underlying assumption of this memorandum is that such integration is necessary for the well-being of the patients, but it is also recognized that it will be to the advantage of the whole staff, in that their personal attitudes are involved in the way they carry out their tasks. There is an attempt to give a really practical description of the pastoral ministry in the hospital, and then follow a number of suggestions about ways in which such integration could be encouraged. In what follows I will occasionally make use of this material.

We are concerned now with the oiling of the machinery of co-operation. What do we need to watch out for? There is a problem here, of which we are normally only vaguely aware, but which I believe to be more significant than it is often thought to be. It is not even discussed in the memorandum. It is that the

minister can also represent a threat to the staff. The embarrassment and resistance noted by Barnes spring not only from the
fact that the staff do not understand what the minister is doing
but also that, not understanding, they are afraid that he may do
something wrong. The medical and nursing staff are responsible
for the patients entrusted to their care. They have the power
to subject all those who appear at the beds of their patients to
certain rules, which make proper oversight of the situation
possible and help them to prevent mishaps. Yet the minister
falls outside this authority. Not infrequently that raises anxious
questions. What does he do with and, much more pertinent, to
the patient? One has the feeling that he is moving in territory
in which the final word lies with the doctor or nurse, but one
cannot see where he fits in, and whether he can be controlled.
This can lead to considerable difficulties, where he is dealing
with temperamentally unstable patients. There is no blueprint
solution. One can only appeal to realism and good humour on the
part of both parties involved. We will only make some progress
if we recognize that such situations do occur and can be demonstrated. Where there is an awareness of the need to work together
and a proper respect for each other's independence, such problems
must be capable of solution.

It should be clear that the integration of the pastoral ministry
into the life of the hospital can create uncertainty and tension.
In this situation the minister should find it possible to fulfil his
task in a satisfying manner if on the one hand he manages not
to lose sight of his distinctive 'order', his own 'wavelength',
while on the other hand he knows himself to be held in a positive
relationship both with the patients and the staff. There are some
useful suggestions in the memorandum. We find some detailed
answers on the question of what kind of thing we may expect
from one another. Priority is given to the answer that we are right
to expect understanding of each other and support in carrying
out our respective tasks: we should strive, within certain limits
such as that of professional secrecy, to make one another's work
possible. However, the memorandum goes further and argues

that this requires good *contact*. The minister must be interested
in the work of the medical staff and in them as persons. This will
mean visiting the medical men in their offices, taking part in social
events, cultivating interest in medical demonstrations, etc. The
memorandum rates the status of the minister on the level of that
of the medical staff. At the same time, the minister has a personal
responsibility towards the highest and the lowest placed in the
hospital hierarchy, always remembering that they are likely to
have links with churches outside the hospital. Hence he must
get to know them as well as may be and try to help where he
can (e.g. in personal matters or in helping with some course).

I consider it important that there is such a clear emphasis
on the contribution the minister can make towards the smooth
running of the set-up. He is a member of the team. In practice
this means that he is a member of a small community, that of the
whole staff. Wherever possible he should 'take part'. Naturally,
the contribution made by the regular hospital chaplain will be
other than that of the visiting minister, but the latter also needs
to be on the lookout for opportunities of establishing more personal contact with the members of the hospital staff, which he
visits regularly. In general, the relationship of the minister
towards the members of the hospital staff must be the same as
that which he has towards the patients. He should also be available to them as a minister. He should be prepared for personal
conversations, and the full-time chaplain could well arrange a
group of junior and/or senior nurses, in which they could
talk with each other about important personal problems arising
in their work. I believe that some such contribution to personal
understanding should be part of the nurse's training. Naturally
a similar group of medical staff would also be useful.

# 6

# The Minister and his Conversations

In this book we have defended a particular image of the minister and his work. It will have become clear that we have drawn the lines rather differently than would normally have been the case in the past. In the life-pattern of the kind of society in which the image of the minister with which many still live today was formed, the minister was the one who proclaimed a certain message and was the representative of a particular morality – he was there to preach and admonish. In this pattern he stood over against or above people: he was a father-figure, one of the many such figures who determined personal and communal life in the paternalistic structures of this older society.

Naturally the responsibility for the proclamation of the gospel and for the quality of life in the community remains a distinctive element of the pastoral ministry, but the accents have shifted in this modern world with its changed structures. The minister is no longer the father-figure of previous days: more accurately, such father-figures are disappearing. He becomes, instead, the companion, the ally, the one who in obedience to Christ enters *with* the other into the problems of existence, so that together they may listen to the guiding light-giving word of the gospel and let it speak to them.

Much of the minister's work consists of conversations. In these his first task is to enter as fully as he may into the other man's world, to accompany him on an inner exploration. It will hold surprises not only for the minister but also for the other, before they finally stand together in the light of the gospel. To use an image of Fosdick, the American preacher, a pastoral conversation is like sailing round an island: you make the best landing when you have sailed right round it. In other words, the message of the gospel will only work when the minister has entered into a real pastoral relationship with the other person. He must have understood him, entered into his world, and he must be with him. Otherwise his conversation will be a more or less authoritarian 'talking-to' from a distance, which is no longer appropriate to present-day structures. I want to emphasize that this understanding of pastoral relationships is not a piece of 'technical advice' based on certain modern insights into the nature of conversations, but that in the simple existence of such a relationship there is a partial realization of the gospel. The minister in his work represents the one who has fully entered into the world of men and become one with them – the basic meaning of the incarnation. In the work of the minister there should be that same movement which we find fully completed in Christ. Our being with the other is a reflection of Christ's saying that he will be with us to the end of the world, one could almost say a realization of it.

Now that we have seen that it is this image of the minister and his work in the hospital that we have before our eyes, what implications follow in practice for his conversations with the patients? This is the question I particularly want to deal with in this chapter.

In very general terms we can say that a pastoral conversation, especially in hospital, involves the minister in a tension – he is both uncertain and calm. Every conversation arouses a sense of uncertainty in him: he does not know the situation of the sick person; he has to enter unknown territory and so to feel his way into the other's life, so that the gospel message will spontaneously find an echo in their contact with each other. He is, moreover, aware of his own questioning in the face of suffering and pain, and certainly in the face of death. He enters this conversation as a man with all the weakness the flesh is heir to. On the other hand, he must not be uneasy towards the other: he must be able to make the other feel that he stands with him. His own thoughts and emotions cannot be allowed to hinder their contact. A sound training in conducting conversations, in which we learn to recognize and accept our uncertainties, and experience can help us in this. Yet at the deepest level it is naturally a matter of the minister's own faith, whether he believes, in the midst of all his uncertainty, that – speaking theologically – the Holy Spirit is guiding the conversation whenever the relationship is sound and not being forced by him into particular channels, and that in that relationship it will also become evident that Christ is with his people to the end of the world. It is in this light that I would consider the question whether the minister needs to know the diagnosis of the patient's illness. Doctors often dislike giving the minister such information. They are faced with the problem of professional secrecy; often they are not too sure of the exact diagnosis; they cannot really see why the minister needs to know; and, let us face it, they are sometimes afraid that he might give away what he knows to the patient.

There are also, I believe, disadvantages to contact between the minister and the sick person. Occasionally some under-standing of the patient's illness and of the likely consequences can be helpful in establishing a relationship. It can also be helpful to have some idea of the seriousness of the situation. However, if the knowledge is sought in order to give the minister a certain confidence in his approach, then this is mistaken. He must approach the sick man with as open a mind as possible; he must be available to react to those things which the patient wants to share with him, and his reactions must not be geared to the knowledge he has gained about the patient from the doctor. If things are right, he will sense that his contact with the patient is being blocked by such knowledge, and the sick person will sense this also.

This also sheds light on the vexed question of 'telling the truth' to those who are sick. We tend to regard truthfulness about the nature and seriousness of an illness as a matter of imparting facts. And yet clearly, for the sick man, truth means much more than that. It can mean a death sentence, the announcement of something irrevocable, given at a time when he is totally unprepared for it. Equally it can also mean liberation, the end of an intolerable uncertainty or the return of open communication with people who – to the patient – seemed to be acting out some ghastly comedy, while leaving him to cope with his doubts and fears alone. Truth at the sick-bed, then, is never something objective, such as the truth tracked down in research and then imparted to others. Information only becomes truth for the sick man when it helps him, gives him some light and drives away fears. It could well be that the lie of the one (perhaps the doctor) could be 'truth' for the other, in that it will help him to die in a more truly human way than the (objective) truth would have allowed. Truth is something towards which men grow, and there will be people who cannot attain the final, and for them too difficult truth. They are those whose eyes – in the words of a godly priest – God shields with his hand, and it is not always given to us to move that hand. Truth is also linked with a man's ability to live in the truth, to accept reality. Earlier on we studied in some detail the way in which people tend to react in the face of approaching death. We saw then that one of the great problems is a sense of isolation. Thus the ability to accept reality, to live in the truth, cannot be divorced from the need to approach together this mystery, which is both threatening and yet holds the promise of peace. Truth seen as an imparting of facts, the passing of a sentence, forces the other man into isolation and makes his struggle harder. But truth understood as both the expression of and deepening of our relationship with him can bring liberation. In time of sickness we may as fellow-beings grow together towards the truth. Hence truth can never be understood apart from the relationship; it rests on our journeying together, on the sharing of burdens.

It is for this reason that I believe that it is the proper task of the doctor to acquaint the patient with the seriousness of his situation. It is not up to the minister! That is how I see it. For the

sick man the doctor is the companion, the comrade-in-arms
Every day he deals with his patient and a sort of medical solidarity is created, in which a growing together towards the truth
may come to birth. This is more difficult in the relationship with
the minister; while he is trusted, he is not in the fight in quite
the same way; he will see the patient less frequently; there will
be less sense of solidarity. It is precisely because he only has the
word at his disposal that his communicating of the truth will
so often be heard as the speaking of a death-sentence. The
doctor, on the other hand, as a wise medical man once said to me,
has in his daily contact and dealings with the patient the opportunity gradually to initiate him into the seriousness of his illness
by gently opening up the truth to him, a little at a time, in answer
to his questions and doubtings. He can talk about the modern
methods now at his disposal and, in so doing, communicate
something of the seriousness of the situation without the sense
of the irrevocable. He can then pursue this line until a kind of
unexpressed understanding grows between them, which brings
the truth nearer without ever making it too hard to bear.

In this the minister has his proper role; he becomes the sick
man's companion and the doctor's fellow-worker. At each stage
of the patient's 'initiation' he may seek with him for the light
of the gospel: he will be concerned not so much with the 'truth'
as with the experience of the patient, who will sometimes be
fearful and rebellious, at other times feel freed and prepared
to face a bad and hard situation. In this way he may at each stage
fulfil his commission to seek with the patient for the will of God
in our lives. We may, using a technical term, say that the minister
must take care always to remain within the 'frame of reference',
the whole complex of thoughts and emotions, of the patient.
Where he does this, he will – at least in my experience – discover
that people faced with the approach of death often have problems
other than those that we, who always think about death from a
distance, tend to expect. A great deal depends here on our
religious education. There are those who, on their death-bed,
do wrestle with the questions of life after death. But there are

also many, who in the face of death are far more ready to entrust themselves to this mystery than we expect and whose concern will be to their relationships with those close to them, or to say farewell to them or again – another possibility – to make up for something (a reconciliation, a debt owed) which they have neglected in their lifetime. It is clear that a great deal depends on whether the minister has learnt really to *listen*. We have already mentioned the 'clinical training' courses for clergy. They are, in my view, a vital part in learning to listen.

At this point I would like to say more about the conversations the minister has with members of the hospital staff, especially doctors and nurses. I have already pointed out in a previous chapter that the minister should make a conscious effort to integrate not only his work but himself into the life of the hospital. I will now try to be more precise. We often fail to notice that the problems of a multi-discipline group affect such conversations. Gradually we get the feel of the problems. Questions of prestige often play a big part here. The members of a team comprising many disciplines, while working together and having a common goal, nevertheless also represent a threat to one another. Is he not trespassing on my territory? Who has the final say in this case? Is my point of view sufficiently represented? Such are the questions which live in the background of communal discussion far more often than members of the team realize.

In his relationship with the medical staff, the minister must realize that the primary task of the hospital is therapeutic and that the work of the hospital is therefore directed to this task. There is no doubt that the minister has his own proper task in the hospital. I trust that this book will have given sufficient contour to this task for the doctor and nurse to see it too. Nevertheless, in fulfilling his task, the minister must never hinder the therapeutic work of the hospital; on the contrary, he will seek, where possible, to provide support for the medical staff. He must be able to discern the therapeutic (or anti-therapeutic) moments which arise in the course of most conversations with the sick.

But he also has a contribution to make in his conversations with the medical men. Without infringing the code of professional secrecy, he will at times be able to provide helpful information, whether asked to do so or not. Where, moreover, a good relationship exists, he may sometimes be able to contribute to the discussion of important ethical issues. With the rapid development of medical technique – transplantation, reanimation, etc. – ethical problems are becoming ever more radical and the questions addressed to the minister in these areas become increasingly sharp and penetrating. It is perhaps too much to speak of pastoral care for the medical staff – we must be careful not to make the hospital into a congregation or a parish – but there is certainly scope for a pastoral contribution.

Where good relationships exist, information needed by the minister will – always within the limits of professional secrecy – naturally be provided. Of course this will all be very much easier for the regular hospital chaplain than for the visiting minister, but for the latter also it is possible to discover ways and means.

An important aspect of the minister's work in hospital is his conversations with the nursing staff. My impression is that this aspect is neglected. I borrow at this point some observations from a lecture to clergy by a senior member of the nursing staff. She explained that the nursing profession in the modern hospital is changing. The nurse – partly through the increase in medical knowledge – carries greater responsibility. Her training is becoming harder; without regular further study she will not manage to keep up. Her relationship with the patient is different from that of the doctor. She is constantly with the sick as people, and that requires a balanced attitude, which she can only acquire and maintain with a certain amount of guidance. In some respects her work is akin to that of the minister. Like him she needs to help the patient out of his isolation, to help him cope with his disability, to care for him in his dying (at this point it is the doctor's task to maintain the relationship with the family). In all this she will need to overcome her emotional confusion; it would appear that each nurse works through the problems raised here in her own way or fails to cope. She went on to say that because the pressures now are so much greater than they used to be, the nurse needs someone to talk to. Clearly she was seeing this as a need clergy amongst others could meet. She mentioned as a specific task for clergy a ministry to student nurses; discussion groups are needed here.

She suggested that theological students should, during their training for the ministry, spend some time working in a hospital, in order to get the 'feel' of the place, to learn to understand being sick and sickness of various kinds and to be confronted with the personal problems involved. Finally she stressed that, if the minister wanted to fulfil his task properly, he should take pains to cultivate good relationships with various members of the hospital staff. My impression is that she displayed a good grasp of the pastoral ministry in the hospital. We will have to gain a clearer understanding of our role in the hospital partly by better preparation for this task and partly by learning to see that in the hospital the minister must be someone who is available, not only for the patients but also for the staff and not least for the nursing staff. By fulfilling his proper role he can make an important contribution to their work. This can only be done through the growth of good, natural relationships: it cannot be forced.

# Pastoral Care of Patients with Psychosomatic Illnesses

It is with some hesitation that I write this series of comments. It is true that there is probably hardly any illness which is not in some way affected by the personality of the sick person. On the other hand, the causes of any illness are manifold, and this is just as true of psychosomatic illnesses. The psyche is but one cause *beside* others, and this should make us beware of over-simplified diagnosis. The examples I am discussing here are obviously typical cases; in real situations we would recognize some traces more clearly and some less so. Moreover, we do well to remember that the psychosomatic hypothesis is a working hypothesis, which does not hold good in every instance and is not necessarily understood in the same way by every medical practitioner. The value to me of this way of understanding illness as psychosomatic has been primarily that in my pastoral contact with certain patients I have tried to 'listen' even more carefully, because I have known that they were perhaps having to cope with special difficulties.

## I. INTRODUCTION

Psychosomatic illnesses are illnesses in which we know or suspect that the origin and course of the physical illness are largely or entirely determined by psychic factors. In the last few decades a great deal of work and study has been done in this field, resulting in a considerable increase in our insight into a hitherto dimly understood relationship. In our pastoral work we are likely to come across such patients quite often; frequently they are chronic patients with whom we may well be in contact for several weeks. Nevertheless, one finds very little on the care of such patients in literature about the pastoral visiting of the sick. I hope, therefore, in these articles to be of some service to my colleagues, but I must emphasize that what I am offering must be regarded as exploratory and provisional.

## Delineations of illnesses

The list of illnesses in which research has been undertaken into the special influence of psychic factors is still growing. Those which we are likely to encounter frequently in pastoral work are gastric ulcers, coronary thrombosis, high blood pressure, rheumatoid arthritis, tuberculosis, asthma. It has been discovered that certain types of personality react to certain types of 'stress situation' with certain types of illness. The background to this is that body and mind form a unity in which each influences the other. In a sense we have always known this. In practice we accept the fact that you cannot walk along a straight line with a befuddled brain or that nerves at the prospect of an examination are likely to make you feel sick. Hence the GP and popular wisdom, with their practical understanding of people, had a pretty clear idea about the cause of a gastric ulcer when they put it that the patient had had to 'stomach' too much. Behind tuberculosis they divined love-sickness, a wasting away for a lost love or a broken engagement. Sharp sober understanding of people has led many a woman to recognize just as well as the doctor that sick people can be 'naughty' and that illnesses seem to fit remarkably well into the personalities and life history of the patient. What has happened in these past years is that psychosomatic medicine has not only confirmed this practical wisdom and understanding, but has also formulated a theoretical basis for understanding it. We have gained a deeper insight into the kind of personality which is liable to such illnesses and into the kind of stresses which lead to the eruption of the illness. People who suffer from a psychosomatic type of illness are generally people who have not been able to learn to express their emotions adequately in life and who in consequence are more or less forced to express them through their body. Generally we describe the personality liable to contract such an illness as 'neurotic'. The neurotic personality is in fact someone who habitually suppresses unpleasant emotions. He cannot cope with them in an adequate fashion and, therefore, suppresses them. Such suppression is something which all of us do to a greater or lesser extent and something which in our Western world we are forced to do. This explains why the conflicts of such patients appear so familiar to us and why we see them so often in our daily surroundings. In a sense we are all to a certain extent neurotic: we may say that a neurosis is due to the intensification of a normal aspect of life.

Let me try to shed some light on this with a simple example. A man at the office is hauled over the coals by his boss and, because it is his boss, cannot vent his fury on him. He has got to swallow it; to 'stomach' it. Perhaps he can get rid of his fury by slamming a door once he is outside the boss's office, or by swearing lustily. But very often even that won't work, or he may have been taught from his youngest years not to do so. Thus he has to carry it around with him. If this happens too often, or if he feels it particularly badly, then – in popular parlance – it 'makes him sick'. In other words, his suppressed aggression seeks a way of expressing itself through his body. When a man's emotions cannot be adequately given vent to and are blocked, they will be redirected towards the body. Anger, for instance, stimulates our gastric juices, and suppressed and continuously festering anger will continuously stimulate such juices, thus causing a gastric ulcer. The excess of gastric juice attacks the wall of the stomach, thus contributing to the formation of the ulcer.

The stress situation is, therefore, one in which a man is placed in a position of excessive tension, from which he cannot escape.

Professor Groen, one of the pioneers of psychosomatic medicine in the Netherlands, argues that in former times people could get rid of their stressed emotions at the many fairs and the like that used to take place. As these have now virtually disappeared, we need to look for other ways. We encourage people to talk about their emotions and problems. In this way they can get rid of them. Doctors are now sometimes trained specially in conversation techniques with this sort of patient. Research has shown that the neurotic personality is usually formed in the first years of life. A child is at this stage not allowed to, or not able to express his emotions properly, and this gradually becomes a more or less compulsive reaction which it is very difficult to lose. For this reason it is sometimes necessary to bring the problems of these early years into the open.

For the time being I will confine myself to these general remarks. When we come later to discuss the particular patterns of illnesses, we can then note and discuss their special aspects.

It seems to me that in our pastoral contact we need to pay particular attention to three facets. At this point I am thinking particularly of patients with gastric ulcers and coronary thrombosis.

First, a sense of loneliness is experienced by the patient. It is true that the sense of spiritual isolation is characteristic of all psychic illness, but in this instance there are distinctive features. Anyone who has an eye for this will be struck by a kind of helplessness behind a façade of courage; such patients are often like big children in their fear, people without support, who used to appear competent and give the impression of being well equipped to cope with life on their own. When probed more deeply, however, they appear to have a longing to be passive and yet at the same time an inability to be so. They cannot really cope with their own problems; they have no one in whom they can really confide; they irritate those around them by their helplessness and feel themselves disappointed in their need of a woman's warm sympathy.

The second point we need to note is that the so-called 'super-ego' is central to their problems. The 'super-ego' is the psycho-analytic term for the primitive childish beginning of the conscience. It has two aspects, forbidding and punishing on the one hand and ideal-forming on the other. In patients of the kind we have mentioned we meet clearly the ideal of being the strong, big, competent man who both can and wants to work well, while on the other hand being forbidden to be small, passive and sick. These are two aspects which play a considerable part in the life of many men and women today. The difference in the patients with which we are concerned is that they have a neurotic character because the two aspects are present in excess and the patients are not able to be objective about them; the aspects have a compulsive character. So the patients are in a sense never without the fear of appearing to be small and yet also never without the secret longing to be small. When we get to know such people better we will, therefore, find a great deal of rejection and compulsion.

Thirdly, we need to note that the way in which they experience their bodies is characteristically involved in their neurotic problems. Little has been written about this, but in our pastoral contacts we will sometimes make some very strange observations. These are people who need their bodies in order to prove their competence, in a sense, to demonstrate their childish achievements to their parents. Now they have been struck exactly at the point of the body. One patient told me: 'I had never imagined that this (coronary thrombosis) could happen to me; I have been in concentration camps for four years and seen others, who were not nearly so strong as I, die around me; I thought that I had a strong body.' Here the body is experienced with a combination of pride and fear. Often with such people we will sense in the background the desire to remain young and a fear of becoming old and of senile decay; sometimes this is accompanied with guilt feelings about a way of life, through which their families have been deprived.

In any case it is usually clear that their illness has shattered their pattern of life; they are no longer able to appear strong and competent; they have to learn to become more passive. It is as if they are being forced violently to learn the great lesson of the second half of life, which Jung has described so strikingly (the need to become more introspective and to see oneself in wider perspectives). It seems to be no coincidence that coronary thrombosis usually falls in those years which Jung marks as critical.

A further point for us to remember is that it is not the minister's task to 'diagnose'. Not every gastric ulcer is psychosomatic, and patients sometimes have a sense of guilt at having an ulcer, so that they would experience 'diagnosis' on our part as a kind of reproof.

## Directions for pastoral contact

At this point I only want to make some general observations. When later we discuss the different kinds of illness, I hope to be more concrete and precise.

Two questions seem to me of importance for the minister. First, what is the situation of the patient in the sight of God? How do we let the light of the gospel fall upon this situation? This is in essence the question of the relationship of neurosis to pastoral ministry. In a patient we may see one who is drowning, one who is helpless and afraid, one who feels he has to cope on his own and who cannot do it, one who feels he does not belong any longer, that he is perishing. In the light of the gospel we must say: that it is not necessary; nobody perishes; you do belong; you do not have to be able to cope; you are not alone. Secondly, what should be our attitude and, in consequence, our behaviour and technique if we are to be able to help and not scare off these people?

To put it briefly, our attitude must be that we not only talk the gospel, but that we *live* and so *bring* it. In practice, this means that we must not become uncertain ourselves; we must not let ourselves be swept up in their uncertainties and become 'wild'. These people arouse our anxiety and uncertainty: we must preserve a healthy distance. Equally we must avoid suggestion and make light of their plight ('Cheer up! It will turn out all right!'); that is only a device for warding off our own fears, a spuriousness of which the sick person is irrevocably aware. We must take their problems seriously, i.e. give attention, time and love. We need to be with them; this gives them some security. This means that we listen, do not criticize, make reproaches or appeal to their 'manliness', but through listening try to help them to be passive and to enter the experience of being accepted. Only within such a framework may we point to the gospel message.

## Warning

At this point I want to enter a small warning. All this can tempt the medical layman to think in too simplified a way about patients. This is, in fact, something the medical profession also tended to do in the early years, though there has been a clear reaction against the initial over-enthusiastic acceptance of psychosomatic medicine. The great expectations engendered in the beginning have not been entirely fulfilled. First of all, it has come to be recognized that every illness should be understood as due to a multiplicity of causes; physical, spiritual and social causes together give the illness its characteristic shape. We may not therefore make the psychic factors absolute. Moreover, we need to realize that chronic illness has its effect on a person; hence certain psychic characteristics may be the *result* of an illness. Thirdly, the psychological problems are often so deep rooted that one has to opt for somatic therapy and recognize that 'talks' with the doctor are a means of lightening the burden rather than an actual cure. If the latter is to be attempted it is a task for the psychotherapist and not for the minister. Moreover, even advocates of the psychosomatic approach are not always agreed about the specific personality-structure and stress-situation characteristic of a type of illness. The minister does well to remember this.

## II. PATIENTS SUFFERING FROM
## GASTRIC ULCERS

In 1947, Dr J. Groen, formerly professor in Jerusalem, now at
Leiden, and at the time working with the Wilhelmina-Gasthuis
in Amsterdam, published a book, *De Psychopathogenese van het
Ulcus Ventriculi en Duodeni*. While it was a first attempt to make
some scientific observations in the field, and later publications
naturally show improvements, this study nevertheless puts things
in a way which can be readily understood and grasped by the
minister.

The gastric ulcer is clearly a physical illness. However, it is
also reckoned to be among the so-called 'managerial diseases',
an indication that physical factors often play a part in causing
gastric ulcers. All of us know those who suffer from this from
our pastoral work. Because they are usually ordered to undergo
a rest-cure, they tend to be amongst those patients with whom
we have more contact than usual. An ulcer in the stomach or the
duodenum can cause the patient a great deal of pain. He has to
be careful with food and knows that he runs the risk of stomach-
bleeding. As we already saw in the introductory article, popular
comment is that he has had to 'stomach too much'. This shows
an awareness of psychic factors in the background. Closer study
has demonstrated that, just as in cases of coronary thrombosis,
it is people with certain personality traits who tend to get gastric
ulcers when under stress. Dr Groen's book is an attempt to make
progress in this field.

He shows how much such people are recognizable by distinctive behaviour patterns, which reveal distinctive character or personality structures. He lists a number of marked characteristics; a good intellect, oral emphasis (eat a lot, talk a lot, smoke a lot), a great deal of industry, a sense of orderliness, masses of activity, abundant energy, strongly outward directed attitude (extrovert), quick reaction to external changes (e.g. in work), the need to be independent, strong sense of duty and responsibility (one notices the clear emergence of the 'super-ego' factor), integrity, scrupulous care in matters of money, a sense of responsibility for the family, social awareness, overloading oneself with work, worry about the future, ambitiousness, a self-assured manner, a competitive spirit, strong feel for hierarchy, respect for women.

The features which stand out in this summary and are underlined by the more detailed explanation offered by Dr Groen with each characteristic, are marked conscientiousness (the 'super-ego'), a compulsive busyness, the need for competition (a factor not found with patients suffering from coronary thrombosis), and finally suppressed aggression, a feature found in both. When we study the personalities of these patients more closely, certain things strike us. Groen mentions a measure of mother-fixation, lack of a warm relationship with the father, a strong need for affection and coddling (a characteristic kept hidden in daily life, a feature also of coronary patients), a marked vanity (quasi-modesty), a large almost excessive measure of sensitivity, a hidden egotism under the guise of social responsibility (the desire to receive praise for doing good), lack of courage to say 'no' (cf. coronary patients!), and an inner tension. Thus we sense in the deeper layers of the personality an unmistakable uncertainty and tension. These are unintegrated people who have difficulty in coping with life. Groen adds two important character traits which give further depth to the picture. Such people try to appear strong; they are ashamed to exhibit their deeper emotions. They *have* to appear calm and self-controlled. At the same time, for such people failure is very hard to bear and to digest. They find themselves prey to feelings of resentment and enmity towards those who stand in their way. Thus they will accuse and blame themselves. Every failure is seen at once as an attack on their self-respect.

### Need for love

In the picture which we have built up in this way, there are certain similarities to coronary patients, but the latter are nevertheless different. We do not, for example, find in them the suppressed aggression against 'rivals'. Nevertheless, what stands out in both personalities is the need for a woman's love, the need to be allowed to be passive, a need which is hidden behind a façade of activity and strength.

One might well ask why people are like this. Can they not learn to live in a different way? The extraordinary thing is that one can discuss this very successfully with such patients and that they can obviously show understanding, while at the same time one senses in the background of their existence a kind of 'compulsion' from which they find it extremely hard to escape. Deeper psychoanalysis often reveals that this is due to conflicts experienced at an early age and not solved at the time, emotions which could not be brought to the surface and were then suppressed. Thus we find that the root cause of a physical illness here is a neurotic personality, and often help can already be afforded when the patient can find someone he trusts sufficiently with whom to talk through the actual conflict.

Groen says that an ulcer is formed, when (*a*) self-expression through work does not meet with success; (*b*) the possibility is lacking of being the passive recipient of love; (*c*) the patient has to or wants to cope with his difficulties 'internally' and reacts to the situation with the familiar characteristic double-edged emotions. In other words, the patient experiences failure in his conflict; he suppresses his aggression; he cannot 'cry his heart out' to an understanding person and hence tries to 'stomach' it himself; then the aggression, which is not able to come out along normal paths, in a sense redirects itself inwardly. We have already said in our article that suppressed aggression leads to a more or less permanent production of gastric juices, which after a while begin to attack the wall of the stomach and so cause an ulcer. Groen gives us in his work several examples of patients in whose history one can see this progression quite clearly. So long as a man who reacts with aggression to a conflict situation finds in this situation an understanding and accepting person, nothing happens. When such a person is lacking in one way or another, gastric complaints emerge.

I imagine that in this picture we are likely to recognize people we know and may even get glimpses of ourselves. This is not surprising. In patients with ulcers, in fact in many neurotic personalities, we recognize magnified versions of the normal. There is in every person's life a tendency to meet danger and failure with 'a stiff upper lip' and not to give ourselves away; we all experience the tension between the desire to be active and to find our strength there and the desire to be passive, the need for protection and understanding. These are behaviour patterns which we often find in their purest form in children. The neurotic personality is one which, when tension arises in his experience, is not strong enough to react in an adult way and falls back on childish patterns. What is wrong, therefore, is not that the sick person falls into such behaviour patterns, but that he seeks his salvation in these too readily and too often. Thus he needs not only physical help, but also spiritual help (psychotherapy).

## Pastoral directions

We tend to meet patients with ulcers fairly frequently in our work. What should be our attitude towards them? In the first place we must be careful not to arouse aggression in them. We are likely to do this when – often with good intentions – we criticize the patient or play down his complaint and his behaviour. Against us also he has no defence, and this situation makes him ill. The patient longs (and this is our second direction) for understanding: we must listen to him and seek to make him speak openly. The third contribution we can make is so to 'go with' him that we arrive at some understanding of his life. Many patients see us as people who have a certain wisdom about life because of our calling, an understanding of the fundamental distortions of life and a proper approach to life. But we must be careful here. We must try to pump something into a patient. What really helps is the discovery which the sick man in a sense makes for himself as we talk together. It is our task to go with him on this journey of discovery. A fourth task is through our words, and even more through our whole attitude and faithfulness in visiting him, to help him sense that he also belongs to God's family, that he therefore does not stand alone, but that he is in a milieu in which he is accepted and where he may be passive.

We have more opportunity of pastoral contact with such patients than with those suffering from coronaries, in that we will be able to talk with them frequently, while there is seldom any real threat to life. One or two warnings. The patient will try to appear brave, but we should beware of childish characteristics and needs. Nor must we forget that the 'cantankerous nagging' of an ulcer also has its effect on the psyche. Finally, we must not forget that an ulcer can also be due to perfectly normal physical causes, e.g. excessive use of aspirin.

# III. PATIENTS WITH CORONARY THROMBOSIS

A medical study which is important for us is a book published by a group of Dutch doctors, *Het acute Myocardinfarct, een Psychosomatische Studie*.[1] Coronary thrombosis is a physical illness which is fairly closely linked with our modern, Western way of life; it was, for example, not found at all amongst Jewish immigrants to Israel from the Yemen until some time after immigration. It is an illness which affects the coronary arteries of the heart, a thrombosis which appears quite suddenly. There are probably several different causes, such as calcification, high blood pressure, heredity, too much fat, a lot of smoking, little movement. The fundamental cause of the appearance of a coronary thrombosis is not established. There is, however, a clear indication that certain psychic factors also play a part. Those who succumb tend to be 'manager-figures', people who react to certain conflicts with certain patterns of behaviour. I will point out some factors which are discussed extensively in the book above.

First, the personality structure. An American patient sketched this out in a striking way when he described the conditions of membership of the 'coronary club'.

1. Your job comes first; personal considerations are secondary;
2. Go to the office evenings, Saturdays, Sundays, and holidays;
3. Take your briefcase home on the evenings when you do not

go to the office. This provides an opportunity to review completely all the troubles and worries of the day;

4. Never say NO to a request – always say YES;

5. Accept all invitations to meetings, banquets, committees, etc.;

6. Do not eat a restful, relaxing meal – always plan a conference for the lunch-hour;

7. Fishing and hunting are a waste of time and money – you never bring back enough fish or game to justify the expense;

8. It is a poor policy to take all the vacation time that is provided for you;

9. Golf, bowling, billiards, cards, gardening, etc. are a waste of time;

10. Never delegate responsibility to others – carry the entire load at all times;

11. If your work calls for travelling – work all day and drive all night to make your appointment for the next morning.

These conditions were worked out by a patient during convalescence after a heart attack.

We are dealing here with 'workers', 'fighters', 'leadership' figures, people who like patients with ulcers, have often had to cope with authority conflicts in childhood, people with a certain kind of optimism (yet with an undercurrent of fear and uncertainty), domineering personalities. What strikes one, though, is that everything is excessive.

It appears that a coronary thrombosis often occurs at a time of conflict, in which it is noticeable that the patient was confronted with the threat of failure, 'defeat', in financial affairs, at home with wife and children, or at work. But patients were often men who had then sought support from other women. Their behaviour in such conflict situations was also strikingly similar. They tended to keep silent about their difficulties and had begun to work even harder; they clearly did not want to show any 'fear' and kept up the appearance of strength; they were often men who had had a hard childhood, in which they had known much deprivation. Often such men did not feel themselves 'understood' by their own wives. Coronary thrombosis amongst women is rarer, but when women do have an attack they, too, often are such hard-working figures. It would seem that it is often the physical exertion in the conflict situation which causes the thrombosis.

## *A deeper analysis*

When we analyse the situation more deeply, we notice how much of the behaviour outlined above must be ascribed to an 'inner' compulsion. Here are patients who often exhibit the problem of the 'super-ego' mentioned in the previous article. This 'compulsion' is linked with the rejection of being passive, the fear of being powerless. Sometimes we can see this rejection swing over to a search for and clinging to a childish dependence. The extra-marital relationships noted above often have this character. Such patients sometimes say of themselves that while they have a 'big mouth', they have only 'a small heart'. In our first article we pointed out that the suppression of aggression is often a contributory cause in psychosomatic illnesses. Such patients usually cannot cope with their aggression in a healthy manner. They often 'explode', and if they are not able to get rid of their aggression, it often turns inward. They have, so to speak, been good long enough, but cannot keep it up any longer; they 'break down'.

In the man/woman relationship also, such patients often want to and need to appear 'strong'; they have a tendency to dominate, if necessary in an indirect way through 'spoiling'. One of the doctors contributing to the work mentioned above writes:

While the basic attitudes are always difficult to define, one could describe them as compulsively restless and driving, with a tendency to sharp changes of mood from bubbling exuberance to helpless littleness. Central to this is the fear of being small, powerless, broken. One has the strong impression that this is also true before the appearance of the thrombosis.

The behaviour of such people, therefore, seems to be determined by two ideals, that of appearing as strong and big towards the outside, while behind and beneath there is the desire to be allowed to be small. Herein lies their neurotic conflict. Because of this they are afraid of criticism and of coming off second best. As ministers we tend to come across such a patient when he has just had a thrombosis and, therefore, great physical care is the order of the day. For him this is something hard to digest psychically. He lies there quite helpless. He has to be passive and to let others look after him, and is therefore hindered in getting rid of his tension. He is thus really doubly fearful. For this reason he will often want to be active again as soon as possible, and he will very soon be making all kinds of plans. On the other hand, and this may happen simultaneously, he has a strong desire to be 'small' and so to find a measure of security.

### The contribution of the minister

Clearly people who appear at such a patient's sick-bed have great emotional significance for him. The doctor gives him a measure of certainty and security and can help to set him at rest. This will happen, at any rate, unless the doctor is so worried about the patient, that some of his fear is communicated to him. The nurse spells 'mother' to him and the patient will often find it pleasant to be allowed to be 'small' in his relationship to her. Yet, at the same time, it is possible that he may feel a sense of shame at showing himself 'small' towards a woman. How, then, will he react to the minister who appears at his bedside? In the first instance, he will experience him as a stranger who makes him uncertain. Secondly, he will see him as a kind of live conscience, which may make him fearful. In the third place he will see him as a 'friend', one 'initiated', who thinks about such matters, to whom he may be able to open his heart. We must realize that the patient will not find it easy to talk about himself – one of his problems is a form of being passive – hence he will at first probably try to appear 'strong'.

Thus the minister must make it his first task to avoid anything which will make the patient even more fearful. He must try simply to be there, to give him a sense of peace, helping him to realize that he understands. He must listen not only to what he says to the patient, but also to the mood in which the patient finds himself. He must not play down, or be falsely encouraging, or be suggestive, or be critical. He must fully accept the other man. He must also be careful not to give the patient too much to digest. One or two thoughts central to the gospel are quite enough.

# IV. PATIENTS WITH RHEUMATOID ARTHRITIS

In normal pastoral practice we come across patients with rheumatoid arthritis quite frequently. It may well appear surprising that we should suspect the influence of psychic factors in this illness, but scientific research has shown it to be a probability, though we would repeat the warning already given that not all cases are alike. We also need to distinguish between arthritis and arthrosis, which is more a feature of old age. Ministers in their contact with these patients may well have noticed that some of them are in a way 'different' from other people. It is rather difficult to formulate what this difference is. It often escapes us when we begin to try to pin-point it. Perhaps we are closest to the truth, when we say that they appear to us not to be 'quite real'. Are these patients perhaps in some way or other playing a part? They appear in some way to be too good. They are too trusting, too 'pious'.

In some cases we are able to see the influence of psychic factors demonstrated suddenly. During the war a street in one of the provincial cities of Holland was struck by a bomb. Houses collapsed everywhere and people were wounded. In one house which had been spared, several of the wounded were carried inside. For many years someone suffering from rheumatoid joints had lain bed-bound upstairs. When she heard the wounded being carried inside downstairs, she had the feeling that she should not be lying there but had to try to help. She stood up, helped all day and in the evening went back to bed . . . only to find herself sick again next morning. The link-up between the various factors here is not at all clear and the psychological description of this illness is also lacking in clarity, but we are entitled, on the ground of phenomena, to think that here also, as in the two illnesses already discussed, aggression plays a decisive role. The present stage reached by research is discussed fully in a study by two experts in this field from Nijmegen, J. J. G. Prick and K. J. M. van de Loo, *The Psychosomatic Approach to Primary Chronic Rheumatoid Arthritis.*[2] Groen and his colleague, who is at present professor of psychiatry in Leiden, Dr Bastiaans, have also given attention to this illness.

Certain things stand out. First, rheumatoid arthritis patients are often people who control themselves tightly, an attitude in which one is tempted to see a parallel to the emerging stiffening of the joints: they are rigid personalities. They are people – again – with a strong 'super-ego', without flexible human contact, people who on the surface appear to meet setbacks with a smile, who are given to 'day-dreams' in which they themselves play an important part. They are people in whose earlier life there had been a noticeable urge for movement: female patients, for example, were found as girls to have been keen on scrubbing or skipping, while with men, sport had taken a large place in their life. We may suppose that this 'movement' was a form of self-assertion, which we rediscover in their illness. Secondly, we must not, of course, disregard inherited factors as well the influence of climate. Thirdly, we find that these patients in the depths of their life have a strange combination of fear and aggression. One could almost speak of people 'frozen with fear at the aggression emerging from the depths of their being'. Then they are people who have experienced situations of great uncertainty in their younger years: death, marital infidelity, poverty, harsh parents (especially the father, e.g. an aggressive drunkard). The stiffening joints are a kind of safety-providing armour. In the fourth place, we notice that the rheumatic patient needs a great deal of attention (love), for example from the husband or wife to whom they are married. When this is withdrawn, the situation becomes worse. Finally, these are often people who are very precise, over-scrupulous, hard-working, who are nevertheless often fearful and frightened. They are people who sacrifice themselves, who appear never to ask anything for themselves, who are always ready to be 'of use' to others. And yet one notices that they are and act like this in order to obtain 'love'. Their behaviour has a neurotic tinge. It is sometimes a very subtle way of gaining power over other people and so dominating them.

*Life history*

Such people often have a distinctive life history, which both hides and betrays a neurotic conflict. When we begin to understand this, we discover that a line runs through their life history which emerges in their sickness. Put briefly, they are *inhibited* personalities. For the person suffering from this illness, in which one slowly becomes more and more stiff and more and more dependent on one's surroundings, the sickness brings about a conflict; it is experienced in a sense as an attack on spiritual sanity. In a way one sees the neurotic features emerge even more clearly on the sick-bed. Prick and van de Loo suggest that a great deal of the normal behaviour of the patient becomes understandable when we see it in the light of a lack of love in childhood, of which sublimated enmity is a manifestation.[3] If one watches these patients for a longer period it becomes abundantly clear that, consciously or unconsciously, they are trying in a tense way to make contact with their fellow men, but that they are not able to succeed. On the whole they tend to ascribe such failure to a lack of co-operation and understanding on the part of those around them, who regularly disappoint them. In reality it is the patient who is not able to make an emotional link with his fellow man.

We must say, then, that we find behind the description of this sickness extremely unhappy people, who have become involved in a deep conflict with themselves and are not, as a result, able to form deep and genuine relationships with those around them.

## Pastoral directions

Two things have often struck me in my pastoral dealings with such patients. In the first place, they will often act 'piously' in their meeting with the minister. I deliberately use the word 'act', because they give the impression of not being quite genuine; it is a little artificial, a little too good. They are more or less playing a part. They appear resigned, but in such a way that you notice it, even though they do not talk about it. They do not complain, but the pitiableness of their situation is not allowed to escape you. In rather a childish fashion they try to make a good impression. I remember a man who began to recite all sorts of little poems from his childhood. And in literature about the illness I read about the case of a woman who exhibited her great knowledge of psalms and hymns. They quite clearly evoke our pity, but in the strange way of appearing not to ask any attention at all for themselves: they make themselves scarce, but in such a way that you notice it.

The second thing which struck me is that they seem to occupy such a 'central' position. Often they reign in the drawing room. They are more or less enthroned with everything neatly ordered around them; the whole thing has been so well organized that one is almost tempted to think it has been staged. Normally I have visited such patients at home, and I therefore have little experience of them in hospital. It is unlikely that they would be able to organize their surroundings there in quite the same way. At home they often exercise a hidden tyranny. I know of men who for years and years sat at home evening after evening with a sick wife, and of married children who came to visit their mother for a couple of hours every afternoon.

I realize that this picture sounds rather negative. However, we must remain sensitive to their conflicts and the need to cope with their unhappy situation. They have a real right to our positive attention. Letters which I received as a result of this article showed how such people suffer under this conflict in the depths of their being. It is precisely our positive attitude which can help them here. Nevertheless, I have always found real pastoral work with such patients very difficult. I personally have never managed to solve the sort of problems with which such patients confronted me, in a manner which has satisfied me. Their deep-lying conflict (their fear and aggression) are beyond our reach. Hence one is almost forced to join in their game, to accept their 'piety' and 'resignation' as real. I should be grateful for experiences from colleagues who are able to show ways in which we can give better pastoral care to them.

# V. PATIENTS WITH ASTHMA

In our congregations we always find some people who suffer from asthma to a greater or lesser degree. It is fairly widely recognized, and was recognized early on, that psychic factors play a part in the emergence of asthma attacks. There are also clearly *physical* aspects: e.g. some attacks of asthma are brought on because people are allergic to some substance or other. One suspects that there is a link between the various factors, but research in this area is not entirely satisfactory. One of the latest books about this illness is that of Clemens de Boor, *Zur Psychosomatic der Allergie, Insbesondere des Asthma Bronchiale.*[4] Still very readable and instructive is the study by Dr J. Groen, *Asthma Bronchiale seu Nervosum,*[5] and recently there appeared Dr L. J. Mengos, *Asthma-Patienten* (a psychological contribution).[6]

As with the illnesses discussed before, we recognize that asthma also hangs together with certain conflict situations and appears in certain personalities. To the many people who have over the years studied and written about this illness the psychosomatic picture is fairly clear. Groen sums up the characteristics of the behaviour pattern of the asthmatic as follows: independent, energetic, headstrong, egocentric, ambitious, opinionated, irritating, pestering, original, badly integrated, hot-tempered, impatient, over-sensitive, strongly self-righteous, finding it hard to admit he is wrong. This is, therefore, a picture with sometimes some very positive features; asthmatics are often essentially very valuable people. With them also there is, in the depths of their being, a longing for love and pampering. Groen also notes as a characteristic that they are often prudish.

It is fairly widely agreed that the mother is the central figure in the life of the asthma patient. On the one hand she is very loving, but on the other hand she tends to dominate the patient and not to give him enough freedom. Sometimes one could speak of tyranny. Hence the patient is characterized by a deep longing for love, but at the same time by resistance and protest against any form of domination. Those who wish to find symbols of the deeper-lying inner conflicts in the symptoms of the illness, speak of an asthma attack as a 'choking' with anger and a 'panting' for life. It would thus appear that the patient is suffering from a mother-fixation in a deeper way. We do not find this kind of fixation with the father. Ambivalence towards him has a normal character. Naturally the picture given here is highly schematic. There are many possible variations. What, then, for these patients is the situation of conflict?

Groen writes about this extensively.[7] In brief it comes to this, that they are situations which for people with an 'asthma personality' are annoying: someone is interfering in their affairs. They have been irritated, they have wanted to achieve something and have failed. The problem usually lies in the area of 'not getting one's way', of the need to fit in and adjust. In this situation the patient will have suppressed his emotions, i.e. controlled them, and this then will usually be succeeded by an attack. It is noticeable that where he is able to give vent to his bad humour, the attack does not come. In essence this stress situation is a re-enacting of the difficulties experienced in childhood when one had to comply and was not able to give vent. Hence such suffering can, just as in the case of a gastric ulcer, become more or less chronic, if the patient permanently has to remain in an irritating situation. Hence also one of the therapeutic measures practised nowadays is to bring together a number of patients in a small group in which the opportunity is given to talk together, i.e. to express the irritation (so-called group therapy).

## Pastoral directions

Some straightforward directions for our pastoral ministry arise directly from these findings. We must be careful not to act in such a way that we 'stifle' the patient, but rather make sure that, when he obviously wants to have a good talk with us, he has the opportunity through patient sympathy on our part to get rid of his bad humour.

On the other hand we should beware, I believe, of dealing in therapy in an amateurish fashion. We are not to be pseudo-doctors, but fully ministers. It seems to me especially important with asthma patients that we do not constantly think about their illness and the reasons for it, but that we make a conscious effort to deal with the healthy part of their personality and treat them pastorally in as normal a fashion as possible. We therefore repeat the warning given in the first article, against becoming narrow-minded in this field.

# APPENDIX B

# Two Conversations

For some years Drs W. Zijlastra and I have been taking students at the Seminary of the Nederlandse Hervormde Kerk in Drie-bergen, 'Hyde Park', for clinical training courses lasting one or two weeks. As part of this course we analyse reports on conversations in which the men had taken part during these weeks, in hospitals in the neighbourhood. The following report of such a conversation is made by a Vicaris who during his Vicariate visited the sick ward of an institution for elderly people. The facts have been altered to such an extent that the people involved cannot be recognized. First comes the actual report, and after that the analysis at which we arrived in the group which discussed it. The report is published with the consent of the Vicaris concerned.

## CONVERSATION REPORT 1

Of the six patients in a men's ward, only three were present. After a short conversation with Mr N, Mr G entered. When I had greeted him and introduced myself, I sat down with him.

V1   I have come to have a chat with you, if that is all right.
G1   Are you going to be ordained soon, or is that some way away?
V2   No, I haven't got that far yet. I have at least another year to do.

G2  We have had some of your boys come and talk to us before. What is it you call yourselves?

V3  Do you mean Vicaris?

G3  That's it. I have come across them for some years now, because I have been lying here for six years.

V4  Do you find you like it if someone comes to talk with you?

G4  Yes, I do. With the people here in the ward you just can't talk. One is deaf, the other can't talk and you can't really talk with the third one.

V5  It is a good thing, anyway, that there are others in the hospital with whom you can have a talk. Or don't you have any contact with them either?

G5  Not very much. Whenever possible I take off to Arnhem on my three-wheeler. I can still get along quite well. That is saying something. I was getting very near retirement when my leg had to come off. Forty years I worked, and then, just when I could begin to enjoy life, this would happen to me.

V6  Still, compared with others you can move around quite well.

G6  Yes, I sometimes compare myself with people who do not live here. After all, they are healthy, aren't they?
    [*Silence* . . .]

G7  That is how we lie here, just waiting for our death. Isn't that right, Dirk? [*He addresses his fellow patient.*] (He was an active churchgoer and would always attend church worship.)

V7  But surely as a Christian you can face death with trust? You say you are waiting for death; that means you are awaited; it means that you are coming home.

G8  I suppose so, but it just happens every now and again that you don't feel quite so cheerful about it.

V8  You mean that there is always uncertainty. However strong your faith is, there are always moments of doubt.

G9  Yes, you aren't always equally sure about things. Sometimes you think to yourself: It is quite a step to entrust yourself to this.
    [*Another short silence* . . .]

V9 Would you like us to read a passage together?
G10 Yes, O.K.; You carry on.
Vicaris reads Psalm 23.

## Analysis

*The opening* The opening of a conversation must provide a structure for both partners in the conversation. The framework within which they are talking together and the point of it must become clear as quickly as possible. We should therefore expect the young minister, now that he is visiting a man whom he does not know in an institution, to make clear in his introduction, what it is he has come to do. It became clear from the analysis that he had already visited other people in the ward, so that there was no need for him to introduce himself and equally no need to explain what he had come to do in the ward. Nevertheless, the question was asked whether the structure indicated by the words 'I have come to have a chat with you, if that's all right', was really sufficient. Does a minister really make the object of his visit clear by saying that he has 'come to have a chat'? Does that give the other man enough to bite on? Would it not have been better if the Vicaris had said something like: 'As you see, I am helping the local minister and making a few visits in this place; do you mind if I come and talk with you?' The word 'chat' leaves the structure of the conversation in an unnecessary uncertainty; it is noticeable that the man reacted immediately by asking after the career prospects of the Vicaris, a subject entirely irrelevant to pastoral contact.

The group did appreciate that the Vicaris had added to his invitation to a chat the words: 'if that's all right with you'. The conversation will only go well where both partners have agreed to take part. We must not consciously or unconsciously 'push' people into contact. The group found greater difficulty with the qualifications in the word 'chat'. In discussing this a problem of considerable importance for our preparation for the ministry came into the open. We realized in the course of conversation that men came from the university with great theories about their office, about preaching, etc., only to find that in the actual contact with people to whom one is called to 'preach' in an 'official' relationship all the great words are entirely abandoned for the word 'chat'. Here is a gulf between theory and practice, between university and parish, a gulf which must be bridged by the minister. What appeared in conversation, however, is that often it proves to be impossible to integrate study with practice, so that one gives it instead a place of its own as a gripping intellectual exercise outside contact with real people. When in the course of such analysis I asked the group, 'What do you do with your theology in these conversations?', the answer was, 'Nothing'. This is not the place to explore this problem. I only want to point out that experience from these analyses shows us that we can no longer afford to postpone a thorough consideration of the relationship between theological study and practice, and more particularly of the possibilities of practical theology as it exists at present, of the need for supervised stages of training and of a thorough 'clinical training'. The chat which arose from the opening goes through to G3. The only point to note is that the man speaks of 'boys'. One is tempted to ask whether this is not a subconscious reaction to the rather juvenile opening to the conversation.

Nevertheless, the man seems to appreciate this contact in a positive way, when as in G 3 he gives a small 'signal' indicating that he would like to talk to the pastor at a deeper level. He says: 'I have been lying here for six years.' It is a sentence which on the one hand naturally appears to follow from the information, that he has 'come across them for some years', but one could equally take it as an invitation to the minister to react to the signal. Good pastoral contact demands that you recognize and react to signals sent up by the other person. It demands that you listen with a third ear to the feelings of which you become aware in and behind the words spoken by the other. The minister is a man who has a measure of sensitivity to such signals. He reacts immediately: V 4 'Do you find you like it if someone comes to talk with you?' shows that with the third ear he has caught the other man's invitation to enter into the theme of 'I have been lying here for six years'.

The man, for his part, reacts immediately and positively. In G4 he lets something of his problem come through for a moment: he appears to be very lonely and to feel a great need for contact. What we recognize here quite clearly is that contact between two people is always much more than an exchange of words, and that someone, who only hears the content of the words actually spoken does not really understand the other person and is therefore not really able to help him.

In V5 the minister reacts to the man he is beginning to get to know. The man has spoken of his loneliness and his need for contact, and the minister feels that something is now expected from him. So he says: 'It is a good thing, anyway, that there are others in the hospital with whom you can have a talk. Or don't you have any contact with them either?' We found ourselves studying this reaction of the young minister in considerable detail: it seemed clear that it revealed the attitude with which he was conducting this conversation. A minister will always conduct a conversation from a certain attitude, a stance or, more deeply, certain convictions about what he is able to do or to be for the other man, in other words a certain – often not consciously recognized – vision of the task, of the identity of the minister. What attitude, then, came to light in the reaction V5?

Clearly the minister wants to help the other man. He wants to show him a little light in this rather depressing situation and thus to encourage him a little. The question which must be asked at this point is whether we really help the other man by giving him such little bits of light. It is noticeable that the minister himself is uncertain: with considerable sensitivity he feels that this bit of light may well not exist at all and that his well-meant help was only a shot in the dark, with no chance of hitting the target. Hence he asks: 'Or don't you have any contact with them either?' What in pastoral contact does it mean to *help*?

Let us try to trace what happens in the relationship between these two men as a result of this reaction by the minister.

When the group began to study this carefully, they discovered some noteworthy points. First, that by saying, 'It is a good thing, anyway,' the Vicaris fails to enter into the feeling of loneliness which the other has laid bare before him, and in a sense rejects this feeling. He is, in fact, saying: 'You do not need to feel and you should not feel lonely, because you have still got other people.' Yet it is quite probable that the loneliness which the man so spontaneously brings into the open may well have deep roots in his life; these roots are laid bare in G7 when the man says: 'That is how we lie here just waiting for our death.' The man must have a feeling that the minister is not really entering into his world, that he is not really, in a deep way, 'with him'. The second point noted by the group was that the minister in this way fails to be genuinely concerned with the man and his feelings, that he is not letting himself be genuinely touched. In a way he was keeping distance here and was giving 'directions' from afar, letting off a 'projectile' without really seeing clearly where it was supposed to land. To use an impressive word: even though it was an attempt to help, V5 was not an expression of 'solidarity'. When the group had discovered this aspect of the minister's reaction, they suddenly saw that this little word, 'anyway', also plays a considerable part in the later course of the conversation: cf. V6 and 7, where the Vicaris is attempting to help in the same sort of way. He is showing a helping attitude, but of a distant kind. It took the group sometime to digest this discovery. A searching discussion came into being about such questions as: What does it mean to help? What is a pastoral ministry? Was another course open here? Where do you end up, if you 'enter into' such emotions? Is it not your task to lead the other man to the gospel?, etc.

During the discussion, it appeared that our first reaction to the 'need' of another person is to try to 'help him' by doing something, by some piece of advice, or encouragement, or similar communication, what in psychology is called 'direction'. It would appear that this is not essentially help. Hence in certain circles one now hears the slogan that real help is to help the other to help himself. This slogan will not do for the pastoral ministry. One might perhaps even say that the paths of social welfare work and clinical psychology on the one hand, and the pastoral ministry on the other, divide at this point. Pastoral help means in some way or another to bring someone into contact with the gospel. Nevertheless, the discovery that direction fails has a great deal to teach the minister. It would seem that the other man will react in a negative way to direction. Because his feelings are neglected, he feels himself misunderstood and begins to argue with the minister: the reaction, G6, to the minister's 'directive' helping, V6 ('Still, compared with others you can move around quite well'), makes the point very clearly.

To be a minister, therefore, means really to enter into the other man's world, to listen to him with great care, and so to accompany him into the depths of his 'need', that you come together to the point where you both feel that only the gospel can speak here, and it becomes natural together to listen to the gospel. A moment's reflection will show that this view of pastoral conversation answers the question discussed by the group. It should also become clear, that one cannot learn the business of being a minister from books, courses of lectures, or even articles in *Ministerium*, however useful these can be in giving us a clearer light on some aspect. Here we learn by supervised reflection on some piece of work in which we have taken part. Those who have taken part in a 'clinical training' course or have taken part in the analysis of their own conversations know from experience how decisive the difference between these two sorts of 'learning' is.

*Close of the conversation: bible reading*  The Vicaris involved discovered during the analysis of this conversation in the group how very significant the ending of this conversation turned out to be. He found himself able to express feelings which he had probably never put into words quite as clearly before.

Clearly the attitude to the Vicaris changed at V8. In V7 he is still the well-meaning, but 'directing' helper (n.b. 'But surely');

he rejects the feeling expressed in G7 and therefore receives a negative reaction from the other ('I suppose so, but . . .'). However, in V8 he seems to have found such sympathy with the other that without further ado he enters into his world ('You mean that there is always uncertainty. However strong your faith is, there are always moments of doubt.'); he gets across to the other man that he really is 'with him' and wants to understand him fully. It is significant that the other man immediately reacts positively; he has no need at all to discuss or argue, but simply says what is in his heart. What he was saying in G8, 'that you don't feel quite so cheerful about it', he now rephrases at a much deeper level – 'It is quite a step to entrust yourself to this'. Through this change of attitude the conversation has suddenly become a fine example of journeying together towards the deepest need, where the word of the gospel appears naturally. In the report of this conversation we find after G9: 'Another short silence . . .'. The Vicaris, reflecting on this silence, discovered and put into words its significance, a valuable piece of learning. He said that he felt that the man suddenly came very close to him and that he was confronted with a deep problem, before which, equally suddenly, he felt himself become very uncertain.

What is his reaction?

He asks: 'Would you like us to read a passage together?' He thus chooses Psalm 23, a passage which could without doubt in the situation be meaningful to the other man. What is important, however, is to ask why he put this question. Looking back during this analysis he remembered that he did this, because in his uncertainty he did not dare to go any further with this man, and the reading of a bible passage was a kind of self-protection, an attempt to keep the deep problem at a distance. In previous analyses in the group we had already come upon the problem that one of the things one has to learn in the pastoral ministry is to bear and cope with one's own uncertainty. The minister's reaction is understandable, and many reading this analysis will recognize parallel reactions in their own work. We will, however, have to acknowledge that to read a bible passage in this way serves rather to help the minister in his uncertainty than to help the other find a way through his problems. The man's reaction, 'Yes, O.K.; you carry on', confirms that while he appreciates this reading – according to the report he was a regular churchgoer – nevertheless, he does not experience this as a clearly positive element in the situation. It arrives too soon in the course of this conversation: the need in which the word of the bible can bring clarity, light and freedom, was not yet clearly enough expressed. In this way we make it in a sense difficult for the gospel to become 'good news'.

*Final comment* What comes out clearly in this analysis is that preparation for the pastoral ministry includes the need to learn to be a minister. It includes learning to listen (to recognize signals, to gauge emotions, to go with the other); furthermore, learning to recognize and cope with one's own uncertainty, and also learning to let the bible work in a relationship. Such learning is not arrived at through books or lectures, but in a group or perhaps in a discussion of one's work, but always under supervision. The question that inevitably arises here is: 'What are we learning and how do we learn it when studying pastoral theology at the university; in fact, what, in this connection, does theological study mean?' It would seem that there is a need for the theologian and the pastoral psychologist to discuss this.

## CONVERSATION REPORT 2

The following conversation was reported by a hospital chaplain and discussed in a group of clergy. Naturally, the facts have again been so altered that the people cannot be recognized. Mr B is taken by a nurse to a small room, where I am waiting for him. He is sitting opposite me in a wheel chair.

B1   I am afraid I am a bit of a problem, as the nurse has perhaps told you: I am not really a regular churchgoer, you see: I have only been baptized.

C1   The nurse did not tell me this, actually. I hope that it does not bother you.

B2   No, of course not, although I suppose I must be rather a difficult person for you. You see, it is like this. We don't really do anything about this at home. It has only really come about since I have been in hospital. I am in a ward with a lot of believing people. And on Sunday the nurse said to me: 'Why don't you go to church with the others? It'll make a break for you.' So I went. And since then I have been every Sunday. And yet sometimes I think that it is a bit cowardly to be going to church here, because I know that when I am back home later, I probably won't keep it up.

C2   Why do you suspect that you won't keep it up?

B3   Well, it's because my wife really doesn't believe. I know that she would want me to be free to go – she has sometimes said: 'If you would like to go, please do feel free to go' – but, somehow, I find going to church is something you ought to do together, and I wouldn't really like it to come between us.

C3   Yes, I can see your problem. May I give you an example of something rather like it? When I was a Vicaris, I visited a young married couple, where the man was a Roman Catholic and the woman belonged to the Nederlandse Hervormde Kerk. They had both found satisfaction in their church membership. But, now that they were married, they decided not to go to church any more in order not to make problems for each other. But when you began to talk a little more deeply with them, you noticed that this did not really satisfy them entirely – you understand, they had problems either way. What do you think of their decision? Do you think it was successful?

B4   Yes, of course there is the danger that by never going to church any more you end up by losing your faith.

C4   I think so. If a plant continually gets too little water, it won't last very long. However, if I understand you rightly, your fear is not so much how you will work this out with your wife later, but rather whether you are being genuine and honest now, when you go to church and pray now that you need God in your life, but do not turn to him, when you are better again and can cope by yourself.

B5    Yes, that's it.

C5    Then it seems to me that the question which is of importance right now is: am I being honest when I pray to God? Or am I only doing this because you never know?

B6    No, I really do mean this honestly. My faith now is stronger than that first time in church. I also find myself understanding the minister better each time. But it also is so new for me; I would have to start from the very beginning.

C6    That is probably something you ought to think about. As far as your relationship with your wife goes; if you really mean what you say seriously, and later you miss contact with the church and thinking together about it, then it wouldn't really be honest if you kept things to yourself. That is something a marriage need not suffer from. On the contrary, a marriage stands or falls by our ability within it to expand ourselves and in so doing enrich the other. Just in the same way, your wife will have to be herself. And you will probably find yourself learning quite a bit from her critical questions. There is a great deal Christians can learn from unbelievers. And the reverse is true. You would not only not do justice to yourself, but also to your wife, if you did not follow the dictates of your heart. All the same, I am thinking that you would want to do this as much as possible by talking it over with her.

B7    You think, then, that I needn't accuse myself of cowardice?

C7    Certainly not, if faith means something real to you. You mustn't forget that it all seems to come at once, now that you lie here ill and are in difficulties and saw everyone go to church. However, if at a deeper level there had not been an interest already there in you, these things would never really have spoken to you. It is not always necessity that makes us pray. It can also teach us to curse. What has happened to you is that all this has suddenly now become visible and alive. And I don't think that this is only because you are in trouble. It is also because you were alone and, therefore, had time to think. But above all, it is because these things were obviously not strange to you, and in a way they have been woken into life. In that case it doesn't seem to me to be cowardice to yield. On the contrary, it would be cowardice to ignore it all. Anyway, you must think: if the message of Christ has really touched you and set you thinking, wouldn't the real danger of cowardice arise at that point?

B8  Yes, I see what you mean.

C8  Would you like me to finish with a prayer with you?

B9  Yes, that would be nice.

Prayer.

## *Analysis*

We shall not attempt to discuss this conversation sentence by sentence as happened in the group, but only point out certain general aspects which became clear during the discussion. A number of positive features strike one at a first reading of this conversation. First of all, the minister is in no way pushing or threatening. Despite the initial uncertainty which comes through in his introduction of himself ('I must be rather a difficult person for you,' B2), an uncertainty about the way in which the minister will approach him, the patient soon feels at home. The minister's reaction, in C2, to this introduction shows no kind of reserve or criticism; his request for information is rather an expression of interest. In all his contributions to the conversation, he appears to take serious account of Mr B's feelings. He listens to the other and tries to understand him and his problems. In all that he says he appears to be in the 'frame of reference' of the other man, i.e. is with him in his emotional world. His whole attitude is directed towards the other. The whole conversation appears to be an exemplary case of the kind of conversation which in psychological terms one describes as 'client-centred'. From the reactions expressed by Mr B we get the impression that he feels helped and that there is even a sense of liberation (cf. B7).

Nevertheless, I suspect that some people, reading this account with care and attention, will find themselves hesitating slightly. It is not quite satisfactory. Listening to the other man's reactions, one has the sense that he is not really 'with it'. This begins in B6: 'No, I really mean this honestly . . . But it is all so new for me . . .' It comes through again in the search for certainty expressed in B7: 'You think then . . .'. One can sense it behind the rather cool tone of B8 (after the rather emphatic language of C7), 'Yes I see what you mean', and the somewhat flat feeling of B9, when the pastor has asked him whether he would like a prayer together: 'Yes, that would be nice'.

If we have a closer look at the words of the minister, we notice that he is always a little ahead of the other man in his reactions, usually a little too far ahead. It looks as if he has seen further ahead than Mr B, and that he is trying his best to get him to the same point. For example, in C4, he says to Mr B. that his real fear is not how he will get on with his wife, but whether he is being really honest. When the other man agrees, the minister in C5 immediately draws the conclusion which must follow from this. In C6 he starts to lecture the other man about his marriage, and then in C7 he is clearly forcing him in a particular direction. Twice in this passage we notice at critical points the words 'you must . . .'. One gets the impression that the other man cannot genuinely come 'with him' precisely because of this pressure. This conversation is, therefore, not truly completely 'client-centred'. We observe a certain amount of pushing on the part of the minister and a tendency to interpret, instead of listening to the feelings of the other man.

What do we see in this conversation?

We see a minister who wants to help the other man who sits opposite him. But apparently he sees in that other person someone who cannot help himself and who, therefore, needs *to be* helped. The other is 'small', sick and, in a certain sense, powerless. The minister is the one who knows, who understands, who takes responsibility upon himself. Without doubt the minister is a sympathetic personality. But is the other man here not treated too much as an 'object' of our pastoral care? Has the minister not yielded too much to his own need to minister, about which we spoke in chapter 2? Has he not identified himself overmuch with the atmosphere of the hospital? We can see from this report how difficult it is for the minister in a hospital to maintain a proper attitude.

# NOTES

## Preface

1. Elizabeth Barnes, *People in Hospital*, Macmillan 1961, p. 97.

## Chapter 1

1. In: Michael Banton (ed.), *Anthropological Approaches to the Study of Religion*, Tavistock Publications 1966, pp. 19f.
2. A. Querido, *Godshuizen Gasthuizen*, Amsterdam 1960.

## Chapter 2

1. W. Engelen, 'Een sociologisch Onderzoek over Ziekenhuispastoraat', *Bulletin voor pastorale Psychologie*, March 1968.
2. Penguin Books 1964.
3. J. Winkler Prins, *Huisarts en Patiënt*, Meppel 1966, p. 69.
4. Cf. D. Jacobs, *Het psychiatrisch Centrum*, Lochem 1968.

## Chapter 3

1. Georges Simenon, *The Patient*, Penguin Books 1968.
2. J. J. C. B. Bremer, *De Ziekenhuispatient*, Nijmegen-Utrecht 1963; the quotation here is from pp. 55f.
3. *De Invloed van psychische Factoren op het Ontstaan en Beloop van Longtuberculose*, Amsterdam 1952, p. 86.
4. H. C. Rümke, *Studies en Voordrachten over Psychiatrie*, Amsterdam 1943, p. 205.
5. F. Delhez, *De Kunst van Ziek Zijn*, Huis ter Heide 1929.

## Chapter 4

1. Hogarth Press 1968.
2. France Pastorelli's book was first published anonymously in 1933 as *Servitude et Grandeur de la Maladie*. The passages quoted are trans-

lated from the Dutch version, *Het Lijden een Beproeving en een Genade*, De Tijdstroom, Lochem, n.d. For the English version see the Bibliography, p. 145.

3. Included in *Studies en Voordrachten*.
4. Darton, Longman and Todd 1966.
5. Dietrich Bonhoeffer, *Letters and Papers from Prison*, rev. ed., SCM Press 1967, pp. 196f.
6. H. J. Heering, *Tragiek*, den Haag 1961, p. 17.
7. Karl Barth, *Church Dogmatics* III, 4, T. and T. Clark 1961, pp. 366–73.
8. Hart-Davis, 1963.
9. Inter Universities Press, New York 1955.
10. Eissler, *op. cit.*, p. 311.
11. *Op. cit.*, p. 312.
12. Andre Deutsch and Weidenfeld and Nicolson 1966.
13. Hogarth Press 1959.

*Chapter 5*

1. The situation described in the next section is true of the Netherlands, but clearly different from that to be found in England, where the existence of the Church of England affects the Protestant–Roman Catholic polarization both theologically and in pastoral and liturgical practice. What is said about the significance behind the words and actions of the various clergy holds good for clergy working against this different English background. Whereas generally in the book the word 'minister' has been used for the ordained clergy of any church, there are instances here where it describes the Protestant, as opposed to the Roman Catholic clergy.
2. Weidenfeld and Nicolson 1965.
3. The title of an excellent book by R. Kaptein, *De predikant, zyn plaats en zyn taak in een nieuwe wereld*, Hilversum 1966.

*Appendix A*

1. Haarlem 1965.
2. Assen 1964 (in English).
3. *Op. cit.*, p. 132.
4. Bern–Leipzig 1965.
5. Amsterdam 1950.
6. Leiden 1966.
7. Groen, *op. cit.*, pp. 77f.

# BIBLIOGRAPHY

*Anthropological Approaches to the Study of Religion* (ed. Michael Banton), Tavistock Publications 1966.

Autton, Norman, *The Pastoral Care of the Dying*, S.P.C.K. 1966.

Barnes, Elizabeth, *People in Hospital*, Macmillan 1961.

Barth, Karl, Section of *Church Dogmatics*, III, 4, 'Respect for Life', T. T. Clark 1961.

Beauvoir, Simone de, *A Very Happy Death*, Andre Deutsch and Weidenfeld and Nicolson 1966.

Beerling, R. F., *Moderne Doodsproblematiek*, Delft, n.d.

Bonhoeffer, Dietrich, *Letters and Papers from Prison*, SCM Press 1967.

Böll, Heinrich, *The Clown*, Weidenfeld and Nicolson 1965.

Bremer, J. J. C. B., *De Ziekenhuispatient, Nijmegen–Utrecht* 1963.

Bowers, M., *Counseling the Dying*, Nelson, New York 1964.

Buskes, J. J., *Waarheid en Leugen aan het Ziekbed*, Amsterdam 1964.

Camus, Albert, *The Plague*, Penguin Books, n.d.

Choron, Jacques, *Death and Western Thought*, Collier-Macmillan 1963.

Cohen, Gerda L., *What's Wrong with Hospitals*, Penguin Books 1964.

Eissler, K. R., *The Psychiatrist and the Dying Patient*, Inter Universities Press, New York 1955.

Erikson, Erik H., *Young Man Luther*, Faber 1959.

Faber, H., *Over Ziek Zijn*, Assen 1956.

    *Problemen rond het Ziekbed*, Assen 1959.

    *Pastorale Verkenning*, den Haag 1958.

    *Pastoraal Psychologische Opstellen*, den Haag 1961.

    *Pastoral Care and Clinical Training in America*, Arnhem 1961.

    with E. Van der Schoot *Het Pastorale Gesprek*, Utrecht 1966.

Feifel, Herman (ed.), *The Meaning of Death*, McGraw Hill 1959.

Freud, Anna, *The Ego and the Mechanisms of Defence*, Hogarth Press 1968.

Freud, Sigmund, *Totem and Taboo*, Routledge and Kegan Paul 1950.
*Beyond the Pleasure Principle*, Hogarth Press 1961.
*The Future of an Illusion*, Hogarth Press 1962.
Fromm, Erich, *Psychoanalysis and Religion*, Gollancz 1951.
Fulton, Robert (ed.), *Death and Identity*, Wiley and Sons 1965.
Gorer, Geoffrey, *Death, Grief and Mourning*, Cresset Press 1965.
Hamilton, William, *The New Essence of Christianity*, Darton, Longman and Todd 1966.
Heering, H. J., *Tragiek*, den Haag 1961.
Hinton, John, *Dying*, Penguin Books 1967.
Jacobs, D., *Het Psychiatrisch Centrum*, Lochem 1968.
Jaspers, Karl, *Philosophie II; Existenzerhellung*, Berlin 1956.
Kaptein, R., *De Predikant*, Hilversum 1966.
Menninger, Karl, *Man Against Himself*, Hart-Davis, 1963.
Otto, Rudolf, *The Idea of the Holy*, Penguin Books, n.d.
Pastorelli, France, *The Glorious Bondage of Illness*, Allen and Unwin 1936.
Poslavsky, A., *Voordrachten over medische Psychologie*, Utrecht 1956.
Querido, A., *Goshuizen Gasthuizen*, Amsterdam 1960.
*The Development of Socio-Medical Care in the Netherlands*, Routledge and Kegan Paul 1968.
Rahner, Karl, *On the Theology of Death*, Freiburg 1961.
Rilke, Rainer Maria, *Notebook of Malte Laurids Brigge*, Hogarth Press 1959.
Abbing, P. J. Roscam, *Pastoraat aan Zieken*, den Haag 1964.
Rümke, H. C., *Studies en Voordrachten*, Amsterdam 1943.
Simenon, Georges, *The Patient*, Penguin Books 1968.
Scherzer, Carl J., *Ministering to the Dying*, Fortress Press 1963.
Prins, J. Winkler, *Huisarts en Patiënt*, Meppel 1966.

# INDEX